LONE PINE IN THE MOVIES

THE EARLY YEARS: CELEBRATING THE SILENTS

Packy Smith
—editor & publisher

Michael Bifulco
—design & page production

Elizabeth Gulick
—cover design

Don Kelsen
—special photography

CONTRIBUTORS

Richard W. Bann
Robert S. Birchard
Gary Eugene Brown
Ed Hulse
Chris Langley
Duane Spurlock
Karl Theide

Lone Pine in the Movies is published by Riverwood Press for the Museum of Western Film History, 701 South Main Street, Lone Pine CA 93545, in conjunction with the 2015 Lone Pine Film Festival. The contents of this issue are copyright © 2015 by the Museum of Western Film History. All rights reserved. Nothing in this magazine may be reprinted in whole or in part, in any media or format, without prior written permission from the publisher and/or the copyright holder.

Photo and Art Acknowledgments: All publicity stills, movie posters, and lobby cards reprinted in these pages were/are copyrighted by the film production companies that originated the material and their respective successors in interest. The cover photo and "The Oregon Trail" photo gallery" are copyright © 2015 by Don Kelsen and are reprinted here with his permission.

Introduction

by Packy Smith

With this 2015 issue of *Lone Pine in the Movies* we are commemorating the 75th Anniversary of the death of Tom Mix. On October 12, 1940, Mix was driving from Tucson to Florence, Arizona, when his car ran off the road and he was killed. In honoring Mix we are presenting several essays about his career as well as those of a couple of his contemporaries who worked in Lone Pine.

To honor the memory of Tom Mix, the 2015 Lone Pine Film Festival will feature four silent Westerns filmed in the area, including Mix's *Riders of the Purple Sage*. Also screening will be the first feature filmed in the Alabama Hills, *The Round Up*, as well as features starring Ken Maynard and Hoot Gibson. Noted pianist Jay C. Munns will accompany all of the silent films.

Lone Pine in the Movies: a publishing timeline

People often ask about this magazine; how long have you been publishing? How many issues are there? Can we get the back issues?

The first *Lone Pine in the Movies* was published in October of 2003, the brainchild of author/historian Ed Hulse and was intended as a stand-alone souvenir for sale to attendees of the 2003 Lone Pine Film Festival. Hulse had approached friends and Lone Pine supporters who had been researching Lone Pine's rich film history and asked for contributions about various subjects specific to the area. The first issue was a traditional magazine layout, 36 pages, 8½x11, saddle-stitched, with a print run of 300, which sold out at the Festival.

There was no magazine at the next Festival in 2004 and fans who had bought the first were inquiring as to why there was no follow-up. In 2005 Festival Director Chris Langley approached Hulse and the others who had participated in the production of the first to produce an official publication for the Festival similar to that of 2003. So, in 2005 and 2006 *Lone Pine in the Movies* was published for the Festival. In 2007, the Lone Pine Museum sponsored the publication. All three issues following the initial 2003 publication were the same format and were published to coincide with the annual Film Festival. The first four issues, 2003, 2005, 2006 and 2007, were intended for sale at the annual Film Festival and were out of print by the end of that particular festival.

In 2008, for the second time since 2003, there was no magazine at Festival time. In 2009 Riverwood Press, with Packy Smith as Publisher, took over production of *Lone Pine in the Movies* for the Beverly and Jim Rogers Museum of Lone Pine Film History (now the Museum of Western Film History). With Ed Hulse continuing as editor and Mike Bifulco taking control of all layout and design, the magazine was expanded in content, changed to its current 8x10 format and has become an annual publication available year round in the Museum gift shop.

There you have it. The magazine has been published since 2003. This issue is the eleventh in the series and all back issues beginning with the 2009 issue (seven to date) are available through the Museum gift shop.

Contributors to *Lone Pine in the Movies*:

We open with a brief biographical overview and appreciation of Tom Mix by **Robert S. Birchard**, the author of *King Cowboy: Tom Mix in the Movies*. Bob has spent years researching and writing about the early days of American film and is currently the Editor of the *AFI Catalogue of Feature Films*, documenting the nearly 60,000 American feature films from 1893 to the present.

Next we offer an article about Just Tony by **Duane Spurlock**, that originally appeared in *Blood 'n' Thunder Magazine* (Winter 2012). Spurlock, a reporter, photographer and editorial cartoonist for newspapers and Internet blogs as well as a historian and researcher on the history of pulp magazines, gives us an in-depth look at the origin of the story that became the basis of the Tom Mix film *Just Tony* which was filmed in Lone Pine.

Long time contributor **Richard W. Bann** uses *Flaming Guns*, an early Lone Pine sound film, as a springboard to look at Tom Mix's film career with the emphasis on his Lone Pine silent films. He uses a similar approach with *Lucky Terror* and its star Hoot Gibson. While discussing the production of *Lucky Terror* Bann manages to cover the career of Gibson, including the silent Lone Pine films of the cowboy star.

When **Gary E. Brown** ended his near fifty-year career in law enforcement, he was able to devote all of his time to the research and writing about his favorite subject B-Western movies and their cowboy stars. Gary has contributed the story of Tom Mix's last trip from New York to the spot

Tom Mix in Lone Pine, 1922.

on Arizona Highway 89, eighteen miles south of Florence, where he died at approximately 2:15 PM, on that day 75 years ago.

Film historian and writer **Michael Bifulco** presents an essay on Buck Jones in Lone Pine. Mike has been involved in the design and layout for nearly every publishing venture the Festival and Museum have undertaken to date.

Former Lone Pine Film Festival Director **Chris Langley** has been researching local film history for over twenty years. Chris presents an essay on Jack Hoxie who was one of the most popular with the locals of the many cowboys who worked in the area.

This year's cover features Bruce Boxleitner, one of our guests this year, in a photo by longtime *Lone Pine in the Movies* contributor and *Los Angeles Times* photographer **Don Kelsen**. Don also presents another of his "then and now" photo essays, this year Republic's *The Oregon Trail*, a 1936 John Wayne film.

For the duration of the Festival, the Museum will have on display the 1937 Cord 812 Phaeton Tom Mix was driving when he was killed. Robert White, the car's owner, will be on hand to present, in the Museum theater, a program on Mix's last days as well as a history of the car and its restoration.

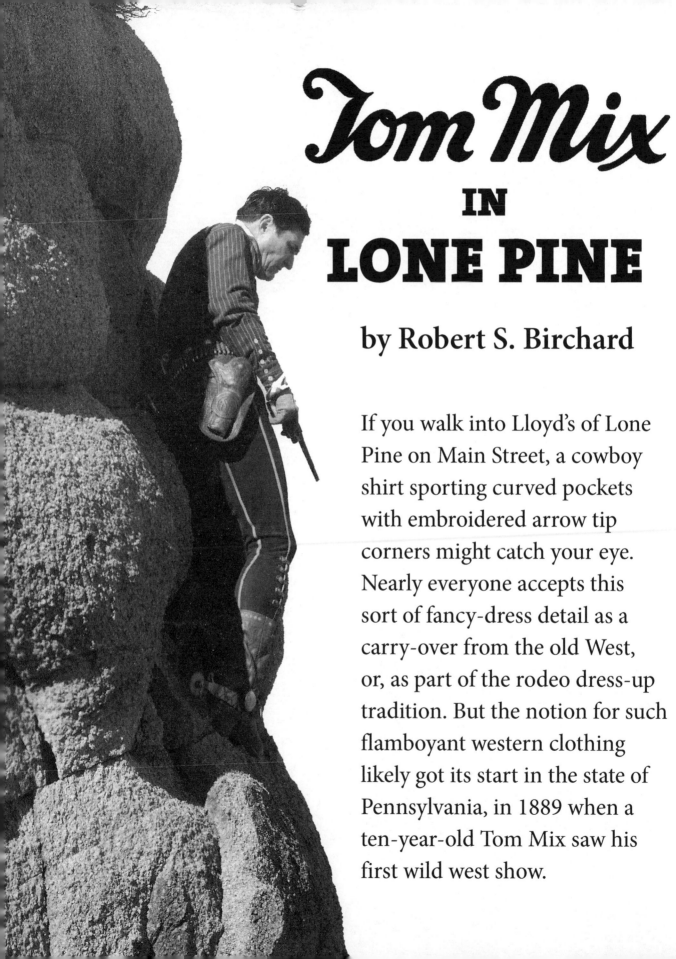

Tom Mix

IN
LONE PINE

by Robert S. Birchard

If you walk into Lloyd's of Lone Pine on Main Street, a cowboy shirt sporting curved pockets with embroidered arrow tip corners might catch your eye. Nearly everyone accepts this sort of fancy-dress detail as a carry-over from the old West, or, as part of the rodeo dress-up tradition. But the notion for such flamboyant western clothing likely got its start in the state of Pennsylvania, in 1889 when a ten-year-old Tom Mix saw his first wild west show.

Tom Mix created what we now consider to be the best Western fashion. Here Tom puts on his tooled leather boots in his dressing room at the Fox studio circa 1928.

Tom Mix kidded his own childhood escapades roping milk cows in the second of his starring series for the Selig Polyscope Company, *The Moving Picture Cowboy* (1914).

"An item I think few people know," wrote director George Marshall in 1967, "is that Tom Mix was responsible for the present-day cowboy clothes. I have been in his dressing room when he was working with his tailor designing the tight-fitting pants, the angled pockets, and the shirts with the many buttons—and always very vivid colors. No question, he was a real showman."

Legend has it that Tom saw the *Buffalo Bill Wild West Show*, but William F. Cody was playing Europe in 1889–1890, and what Tom likely saw was "The only acknowledged rival to Buffalo Bill's Wild West show," *Wild West Life* headed up by "Pawnee Bill" (nee Gordon W. Lilly).

Young Tom was inspired by the, "Indians, Cowboys, Rifle-shooting, the Pony Express, the Robbery of the Mail Coach, the Lynching of a Horse-

thief, the Burning of a Settler's Camp and all the great features of *Buffalo Bills Wild West Show*. Daring horsemanship, startling marksmanship, thrilling scenes of border warfare." So inspired, that when he got back home to DuBois, Pennsylvania, he cut down his best Sunday suit to make his own cowboy outfit. Tom's mother was not pleased. Nor were the neighbors pleased when Tom took to roping their dairy cattle.

Tom's father, Edwin Mix, signed on as stable master for lumber baron John E. DuBois in 1888, and Tom Mix learned to ride hanging around the stable with his dad, but he didn't get his first taste of ranch life until after he deserted from the army in 1902. Tom enlisted with the outbreak of the Spanish American War in 1898, and rose to the rank of Sergeant in the Coast Artillery. Contrary

Lassiter (Tom Mix) rescues Fay Larkin (Dawn O'Day, the future Anne Shirley) in *Riders of the Purple Sage* (Fox, 1925). This film represented Mix's most extended location jaunt to Lone Pine during the silent era.

Stopping for lunch near Lone Pine during the making of *Just Tony* (Fox, 1922). Cameraman Dan Clark leans against the car, then Left to Right: Frank Campeau, director Lynn Reynolds, leading lady Claire Adams, and Tom Mix. Although much of *Just Tony* was shot at Mixville, the film also included Tom Mix's first location work in Lone Pine.

Jane Withersteen (Mabel Ballin) warns Lassiter (Tom Mix) against the evil Judge Dyer, who abducted Lassiter's sister many years before in a tense moment from *Riders of the Purple Sage* (Fox, 1925). The Tom Mix production was the second of four big-screen versions of Zane Grey's 1912 novel. The first starred William Farnum in 1918, George O'Brien portrayed Lassiter in the 1931 version, and George Montgomery starred in the 1941 outing. Ed Harris played Lassiter in a 1996 TV version for TNT.

to the colorful war stories he later told, Tom never saw combat action. When his three-year hitch was up, Tom was honorably discharged. He re-enlisted, but after his July 18, 1902, marriage to Louisville, Kentucky, schoolteacher Grace Allin, Tom discovered that his bride was not fond of military life and, in October 1902, Tom and Grace took their leave from Fort Hancock, New Jersey, and made their way to Guthrie, Oklahoma. The marriage didn't last. It was annulled, and in quick succession Tom walked down the aisle two more times, first with Jewell "Kitty" Perrine on December 20, 1905—a union that lasted little more than a year, and then with Olive Stokes, daughter on an Oklahoma rancher, in 1908. In the meantime, Tom landed with The Miller Brothers 101 Ranch Show

Tom Mix in the Lone Pine rocks in a scene from *Terror Trail* (1933), the first of his second series for Universal.

in 1906 and became one of the star attractions of the show.

Movies beckoned in 1910. Tom would later claim that he was a star from the time of his first film, *The Trimming of Paradise Gulch* (Selig, Polyscope, 1910), but in fact he mostly played supporting roles with long gaps between engagements during his early years in pictures until 1914. His first starring series, beginning with a film appropriately titled *The Real Thing in Cowboys* (Selig Polyscope, 1914), proved he was well suited to being a cowboy star. In 1954, Lambert Hillyer, one of Tom's directors, recalled, "Mix was himself a good man with a rifle, rope or

six-gun. Very fast on the draw, and as a stage coach driver, one of the best."

Mix's early efforts for the Selig Polyscope Company between 1910 and 1916 have to be considered a long-term apprenticeship. The one- and two-reelers he directed and starred in were crude, and not always well staged. His earliest starring films were made at the Bachman Studio, a tiny rental lot in Glendale, California, that did not offer much in the way of wide-open spaces. "I am not making excuses," Tom wrote his boss in Chicago, Colonel William N. Selig, "but I am sure handicapped here [in Glendale, California]

After capturing the villains, Tom Mix send them back to town to face frontier justice in *Terror Trail* (Universal, 1933). Mix shot parts of his last three Universal Pictures in Lone Pine.

for real atmosphere . . . I could easy take . . . what books and stories I have in mind and lay out a years work if I could get back to the ranch country again."

Tom and his unit did set up shop in Las Vegas, New Mexico, the last open range land in the West in 1916, but the fortunes of the Selig Polyscope Company declined, and Mix was soon back in California, first in Newhall, then near East Lake (now Lincoln) Park in East Los Angeles. The distinctly Western scenery he sought for his films seemed more elusive than ever.

As an established star in short comedy Westerns, Tom Mix was signed by the Fox Film Corporation to star in a series of two-reelers for the studio's Foxfilm Comedies series, but the added distribution potential of his Fox pictures soon made Tom Mix too valuable to remain in shorts. Beginning with *Cupid's Roundup* (Fox, 1918), Tom Mix was promoted to feature-length Westerns, though he was still mostly tethered to his own lot in the Edendale district, not far from Glendale. Although there was always more action in a Tom Mix film, Tom's early Fox feature efforts were much more in a serious vein resembling the "adult" Westerns of William S. Hart, who was the most popular Western star in the years 1915-1920.

By late 1921, however, Tom's star power had

reached a level that made it possible to exert a greater influence on the style and subject matter of his films. Although he took more control of his unit, Tom was now content to let others direct his films. Hair-raising stunts, top-notch photography, a more light-hearted approach to screen heroism, and dazzling Western locations became the winning combination that would make Tom Mix the greatest of all cowboy stars.

The first effort in the new mold was *Sky High* (Fox, 1922), shot largely on location at the Grand Canyon in Arizona. Tom Mix would first make it to Lone Pine later in 1922 to shoot scenes for his film *Just Tony* (Fox, 1922), a tribute to Tom's equine co-star, Tony the Wonder Horse. Unlike other cowboy stars who worked repeatedly in Lone Pine, Tom Mix preferred more variety in backdrops from film to film. His one extended location jaunt in Lone Pine would come in late 1924 when he and his unit came to town to shoot *Riders of the Purple Sage*, which was in production from November 7 through December 13, 1924, and released by Fox on March 15, 1925.

Zane Grey's 1912 novel is undoubtedly the best-known Western story title, and it has seen many film adaptations, but it presents a problematic narrative for a mass medium like motion pictures. *Riders of the Purple Sage* is set in Utah during the period after September 24, 1890, when Mormon president Wilford Woodruff stated to the Associated Press, "I now publicly declare that my advice to the Latter-day Saints is to refrain from contracting any marriage forbidden by the law of the land," forsaking polygamy in order to gain statehood, which was finally granted in 1896. The narrative involves un-reformed Mormons who hide their "sealed" plural wives in remote areas of Utah. The novel's hero, the black-clad gunman Lassiter, has spent much of his life searching for his sister Milly Erne who was forced to leave her family and join the Mormon faith. In filmed versions of *Riders of the Purple Sage*, the broad outlines of the story are usually maintained, but the religious and political motivations are ignored or sidestepped in such ways that the narrative becomes muddled. In the end, Lassiter and his fellow allies who have been persecuted by the villains, who are not expressly identified as Mormons, close themselves off from their pursuers in a secret hidden valley, where they will remain for years to come. Because of its somber tone, and its purposely muddled storyline, *Riders of the Purple Sage* is a good Western, but cannot be classified among the Western star's best films. Still, Lone Pine stands in admirably for the rugged rocky hills of Utah. Mix would go on to make a version of *The Rainbow Trail*, Zane Grey's 1915 sequel to *Riders of the Purple Sage*, but instead of keeping the setting in Lone Pine, Mix and company journeyed to Arizona, where the Rainbow Bridge, which features prominently in the story, is located.

Tom Mix would not return to Lone Pine during the silent era, when his 30-day shooting schedules and top budgets allowed location jaunts to places like Cedar City and Zion National Park in Utah for *The Deadwood Coach* (Fox, 1925), Royal Gorge in Colorado for *The Great K & A Train Robbery* (Fox, 1926), the Merced River in California for *Tumbling River* (Fox, 1927), and other spectacular western settings.

Fox failed to renew Tom Mix's contract when it expired in 1928, and he made a handful of lower-budget efforts for FBO [Film Booking Offices] that year before signing with the Sells-Floto Circus for $10,000.00 a week. He would not return to the screen until 1931, when Universal Pictures signed him for his first talking pictures. A burst appendix nearly ended Tom's life before the first of his six-picture deal at Universal could go into production, but the cowboy star recovered and began what is perhaps the second-best known Western story title, Max Brand's *Destry Rides Again* (Universal, 1932). Mix continued to favor spectacular distant locations in his first six films for Universal, such as the desert sand dunes near Yuma, Arizona, for *The Rider of Death Valley* (Universal, 1932), but when he signed for a second six at Universal, the desire to cut costs and the star's battered body after years of doing his own movie and circus stunts forced the Mix unit to work closer to home. Now Lone Pine would serve as a background for parts of his final three Universal efforts, *Terror Trail*, *Flaming Guns*, and *Rustler's Roundup* (all Universal, 1933). The town at the foot of Mt. Whitney is even called out by name as Sergeant Tom Malone (Mix) arrives to visit an old friend when he is mustered out of the Army after World War I, and one of the lady players enthuses to Tom, "So this is Lone Pine." ☐☐☐

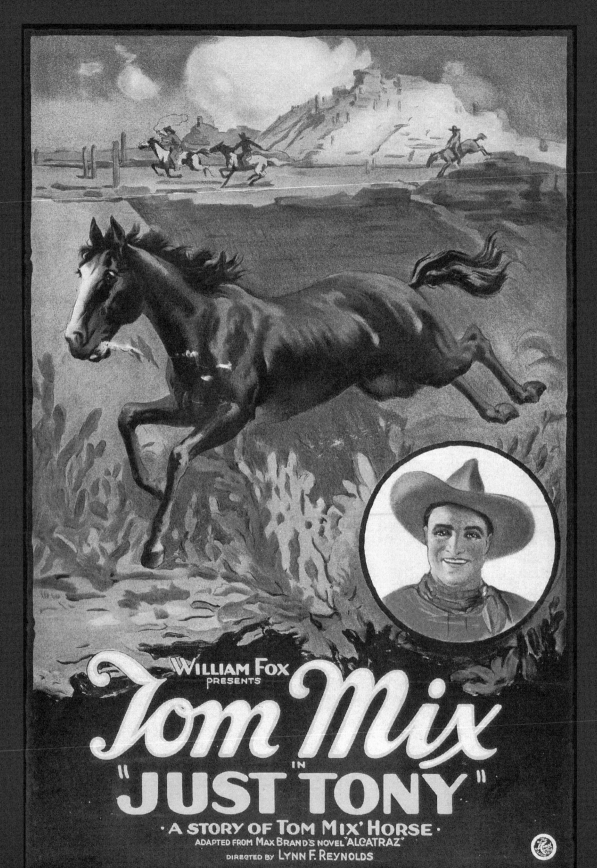

Origins of a Classic Silent Film
by Duane Spurlock

I became interested in translations of Max Brand's stories to film after purchasing a VHS tape at a local flea market. It included two of Tom Mix's silent Westerns: *Just Tony* and *Sky High*. I'd never seen a Mix movie before and thought it was time to fill that gap in my pop-culture knowledge. I didn't realize until I watched it that *Just Tony*, released in 1922, was the earliest movie in my collection to employ that magical place called Lone Pine for its principal location. While watching, I noticed that the credits for *Just Tony* attributed Max Brand's novel *Alcatraz* as the basis for the film. So I thought a book-to-movie comparison was in order.

Frederick Faust's novel *Alcatraz* first appeared under his Max Brand pseudonym as a serial in *The Country Gentleman*. At this time it was a second-tier "slick" magazine, comparable to *Liberty*, but with a lower circulation than magazines like *Colliers* or its sister slick, *The Saturday Evening Post*. Noting that *TCG*'s subtitle was "For the American Farmer and His Family," I thought this weekly periodical might be similar to *Progressive Farmer*, a magazine my family used to receive when I was a boy. After seeing a few cover illustrations and learning that fiction was a regular part of *TCG*, however, my thought changed. Apparently top writers and artists appeared there, among them Erle Stanley Gardner, Hugh Cave, Ben Ames Williams, Zane Grey, John Howitt, and N. C. Wyeth.

Also, the subtitle might suggest that this magazine would not fall strictly within the parameters normally defining "pulp." But Brand has been called the King of the Pulps often enough that the appearance of his work anywhere deserves consideration by the pulp community. Besides, at least one other writer familiar to pulp readers appeared in *TCG*'s pages during the run of *Alcatraz*: William MacLeod Raine's story

Iron Heart began in the same issue that wrapped up Brand's serial.

Curtis Publishing owned *TCG*, and the editor at this time was John Pickett. The serial ran in five issues, from that dated June 17, 1922, to July 15, 1922. For its first installment, the novel was featured on the magazine's cover with a painting by Harvey Dunn. (I have only a photocopy of the illustration, but just from the looks of that poor reproduction, I'm sure the actual painting is quite striking.) The story was accompanied by three illustrations drawn by John S. Curry in each issue except for the first installment, which featured four illustrations.

The cover by Dunn shows that his work is clearly aligned with the American school of rugged illustration founded by Howard Pyle and carried on most famously by N. C. Wyeth and others who came out of the Brandywine Valley school. Dunn took classes there with Pyle. His illustrations capture perfectly the sense Brand imparts in his initial paragraphs—with eagles soaring behind a horse standing atop a mountain (Brand names the ever-present mountains in this story the Eagles), the artist expresses the royalty that the author invests in his equine creation.

A quick scan of the few magazine pages available to me shows evidence that the serialized novel differs from the book version. (I received only a few photocopied pages of the serial thanks to Interlibrary Loan. I compared these to the large-print edition of the novel published by Thorndike Press in 1991. [The first book publication was in 1923 by G.P. Putnam's Sons.]) The magazine version appears to be shorter than the book version. Whether an editor at *The Country Gentleman* abridged Brand's novel or Brand added to the story for book publication is unclear from the limited comparison I can make

Just Tony (Fox, 1922) was made as a tribute to Tom Mix's equine partner, Tony the Wonder Horse, in much the same way that William S. Hart's short, *Pinto Ben* (Broncho-Mutual, 1915) was a tribute to his screen horse, Fritz. Tony on the rocks, as seen above, was used as a live-action main title background for the Mix film.

with these materials. Jon Tuska's "A Frederick Faust Bibliography" doesn't note an abridgment for the book publication, and Faust rarely worked on a story after its completion, so the likely answer is that a *TCG* editor made the changes, or both a *TCG* editor and a Putnam's editor tinkered with the manuscript for their own publishing purposes.

An in-depth textual comparison between the magazine and book editions is not the purpose of this article. But a quick look at the story's first three paragraphs will provide a good notion of the differences that exist in the serial and novel forms.

Paragraph One: The phrase "Arab explanation" in the serial appears as "Arab belief" in the book. "Says the sheik:" appears at the end of Paragraph One in the serial.

Paragraph Two: "Says the sheik:" appears at the beginning of Paragraph Two in the book.

Paragraph Three: The third paragraph of the book starts out with this passage:

Marianne had known thoroughbreds since she was a child and after coming West she had become acquainted with mere "hoss-flesh," but today for the first time she felt that the horse is not meant by nature to be the servant of man but that its speed is meant to ensure it sacred freedom. A moment later [. . .]

The third paragraph in the serial begins with the sentence starting "A moment later [. . .]"

The differences within this paragraph continue between the second and third sentences that appear

In a flashback that establishes Red Ferris's (the character played by Tom Mix) motivation, the drunken Oliver Jordan (J. P. Lockney) takes offense at Red's singing and shoots him. A man with a memory like an elephant, Red Ferris spends much effort seeking revenge against Jordan.

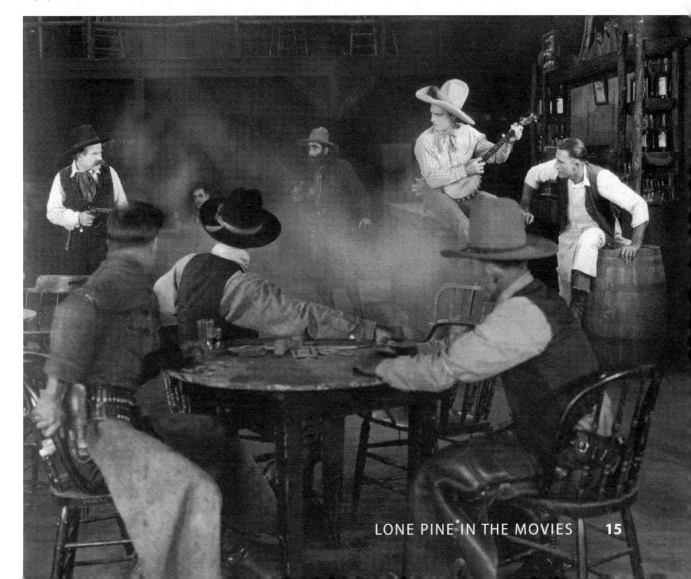

The Bishop, California, Rodeo, which took place Friday through Sunday, May 12-14, 1922, features prominently in *Just Tony*.

in the serial: "That glimpse of equine perfection had been an illusion built of spirit and attitude; when the head of the stallion fell she saw the daylight truth; this was either the wreck of a young horse or the sad ruin of a fine animal now grown old. It was once a rich red chestnut, no doubt."

In the book, between the two sentences just quoted, this passage appears: "He was a ragged creature with dull eyes and pendulous lip. No comb had been among the tangles of mane and tail for an unknown period; no brush had smoothed his coat."

Further differences continue to appear in just this paragraph alone. But the examples I've listed should give you a good idea of the sort of changes made either before the original serial publication or between that appearance and the book publication.

Brand imbues this story, as he does many, with a mythic tone: Marianne Jordan is caught up by the sight of Alcatraz, a horse whose physical form manifests the concepts of freedom and speed. Alcatraz is the epitome of Horse: majestic, fast, untamed and untamable. But he is controlled by a petty and vicious owner, Manuel Cordova, who nearly starves the horse, beats and mistreats him, and races him for the money he wins from those betting against such a worn-looking beast.

Marianne has come to the Glosterville fair to purchase a string of thoroughbreds in the hope of

Red Ferris (Tom Mix) sets out to capture Tony, seeking to force the animal through an improvised chute with a lasso poised to snag the wild horse.

reviving the bloodlines of her ranch stock. She is running the ranch in place of her father, who—following a debilitating injury—has lost any will to take a leading hand at the ranch. Upon returning from the East to take over management, she earned the scorn and resentment of Lou Hervey, ranch foreman, who had been running the spread after Jordan's collapse. Marianne hopes to prove her mettle to Hervey by purchasing the string of blood horses. However, she knows she's pinning a lot on this action: The ranch's fortunes will be ruined if her gamble doesn't work.

Brand introduces his hero in the second chapter: "Red" Jim Perris. He displays typical Brand-hero traits: free and easy, with a desire to roam, untied to any geographical or emotional anchors; he's fair to all men; he's not shy about battling an injustice or anything else he sees as being counter to fair play. Like some manifestation of wild nature itself, Perris has an easy rapport with animals, and even those beasts that seem untamable will surrender to his strength, intelligence, and goodness. And, by golly, he can handle a gun like nobody's business.

Marianne sees Perris in action, and she is both taken and repelled by his cowboy brashness. A sure sign that these two are doomed to romance.

Marianne buys her horses; Alcatraz stomps Cordova seemingly to death and escapes into

Tony the Wonder Horse finds an uneasy home at a corral in the shadow of the Alabama Hills.

the wild; Perris displays his heroic traits and continues on the trail of a man who, in a drunken rage, shot him during a card game and ran off. Unknown to both Perris and Marianne, the assailant was the girl's father. Old Jordan regrets his actions, but Hervey—who was with Jordan at the time and encouraged him to vamoose after the shooting—uses this event to his advantage in retaking control of the ranch and its finances. Alcatraz takes over leadership of a band of wild horses that have been plaguing the Jordan ranch. Hervey and his crew shoot down as many of the horses as possible, but Alcatraz escapes. The crew begins building a legend that Alcatraz is a devil immune to bullets.

Marianne hires Perris to kill the wild horse. This move further galls Hervey. Once Perris sees the majesty of Alcatraz in the wild, he vows not to kill the horse but to capture it instead. Alcatraz

seemingly meets his match when Perris traps him and manages to climb aboard. A myth-sized battle follows, and Alcatraz seems ready to submit when Perris is knocked unconscious after being bumped into a tree limb.

Later Perris saves Alcatraz from drowning, and the horse saves the man when Hervey's crew tries to kill the two. In the end, Perris and Marianne acknowledge their love, the elder Jordan admits his wrongdoing and he and Perris reach a peaceable agreement; Hervey's mischief is discovered and he is banished from the ranch, while Alcatraz and Perris—neither able to surrender to the other—become partners.

Just Tony was just one of nine Tom Mix movies released in 1922, and one of five Mix vehicles directed by Lynn Reynolds (who was to Mix what John Ford was to John Wayne). Reynolds also adapted the script from Brand's novel.

This 70-minute film was shot in the Alabama Hills near Lone Pine, California. The Alabama Hills have been a popular location for shooting movies and TV shows—particularly Westerns—since the filming of *The Roundup* in 1920. It remains in use today. Part of its visual appeal is the Sierra Nevadas backdrop, which includes Mt. Whitney, one of the highest points in the continental United States. Movies shot here in whole or part include *Gunga Din*, *The Three Godfathers*, *Broken Arrow*, *Gladiator*, *Hopalong Rides Again*, *Joe Kidd*, and the 1938 Lone Ranger serial.

Casual movie fans often take locations for granted, but it's significant that Hollywood filmmakers chose Lone Pine as often as they did. After all, this sleepy little town is more than 200 miles from Los Angeles, which means commuting for a day's shooting was not feasible. Producers were required to transport and board their casts and crews, adding a lot to the film's budget. In the case of *Gunga Din*, a million-dollar-plus production, producer Pandro S. Berman actually built a tent city in the Alabama Hills to house the hundreds of extras needed for spectacular battle scenes.

But shooting films in and around Lone Pine gave them a striking visual quality not obtainable in the typical locations scattered around the San Fernando Valley, where most Western exteriors were lensed. Having Mt. Whitney and the Sierra Nevada mountain

In a sequence shot at Mixville, in the Edendale district of Los Angeles, Red Ferris (Tom Mix) thrashes Manuel Cordova (Duke Lee) for abusing Tony.

range for a backdrop gave films a majestic look, and the jumbled boulders making up the Alabama Hills offered innumerable opportunities for picturesque shot compositions and shadow effects (when the sun was in the right position).

In short, Lone Pine was the perfect place in which to make movies based on Max Brand's best Western novels, because the beautiful landscape contributed to their mythic quality. Even though the available video copies of *Just Tony* have been mastered from a 16mm print several generations away from the original camera negative, it's easy to imagine how the gorgeous backdrop enhanced the story's presentation.

Tom Mix was the top cowboy in moving pictures at this time. As a result, his horse Tony was the top equine star in Hollywood. So marketing-wise, a movie named for Tony would surely pull in more viewers than a film titled *Alcatraz*. Thus Tony got the starring role *and* the picture's title.

Mix was perfect to play one of Brand's bigger-than-life cowboy heroes. Tom's background was not that of an actual working cowboy. Instead, he came from the world of the rodeo, wild-west show, and circus-styled cowboy—the sort who specialized in shooting tricks, riding stunts, and fancy-dress clothes (the type of wardrobe we associate with William Boyd's Hopalong Cassidy, Gene Autry, and Roy Rogers). Unlike William S. Hart, Mix's contemporary who supposedly worked to make his Western films look

Ranch foreman Lew Harvey (Frank Campeau) and Marianne Jordan (Claire Adams) seek to prevent Red Ferris (Tom Mix) from taking revenge on Marianne's father in *Just Tony*.

Red Ferris (Tom Mix) warns Lew Harvey (Frank Campeau) that he is on to Harvey's crooked schemes.

authentic, Mix was a true Hollywood cowboy, whose behavior on and off screen was based on spectacle and entertainment.

The square-jawed, hawk-nosed Mix made sure his public image was larger than real life, the hero of movie-watching boys everywhere; he was well suited to portray a mythic character who could have stepped out of folklore as easily as he strode through a Brand-penned novel.

The film opens with a panorama shot of the Eagles, a majestic mountain range in Nevada. Next we see a wild horse herd. Jim Ferris, a cowboy from Utah, admires these fine, free animals. They are led by a four-year-old colt, "a mimic of the desert whirlwinds," according to a title card. Jim marvels at the animal. It could be his dream horse.

But foremost in his thoughts is an account he wants to square. The movie flashes back to a saloon scene. Jim is playing a banjo; a drunk gets tired of hearing it and shoots Jim, then leaves.

The man who shot Jim, Oliver Jordan, later bought a ranch at the foot of the lofty Nevada mountains. Since then, he has suffered an injury to his legs, and the ranch has fallen on hard times. His daughter, Marianne, comes home from the East to run the ranch. Hervey, the ranch boss, is unhappy about that. Since Jordan's injury, Hervey has replaced the older ranch hands with hard characters.

A bad winter kills much of Jordan's and other

Above: Tom Mix and Tony in one of the five pictures he made for F.B.O. [Film Booking Offices], later absorbed by RKO-Radio, in the late 1920s. Below: Claire Adams and Tom Mix pose with Tony in the climactic moment from *Just Tony*.

ranchers' stock. A lot of wild horses are captured as they seek food. One of the captured horses is Tony. Manuel Cordova owns this one-time herd leader. He whips and mistreats the animal.

Marianne, at the local rodeo for stock, sees Manuel abuse Tony. Jim also sees, and he whips Manuel in a fight. Jim recognizes Tony as the horse he saw on the desert plains. He gives Tony "the first caress he has ever known."

At the rodeo, Marianne watches the race that features Tony and the eastern mares she's come to buy. Only if Tony wins will the mares' price be low enough for Marianne's budget. Jim learns that Manuel has bet heavily against Tony and plans to lose. Jim enters the race so "Tony will get a fair deal." Sure enough, Manuel holds Tony back, but Jim rides up and cuts the reins. Tony wins the race!

Marianne offers Jim a foreman's job, for she doubts Hervey's motivations. But Jim explains he has two other jobs that take priority: finding the man who shot him, and somehow claiming Tony as his own.

When Manuel starts to beat Tony again, the horse breaks free, stomps his cruel owner, and escapes to the Eagle Mountains. He takes over another herd of horses, and lures domestic stock from the Jordan ranch, including the newly purchased mares. Marianne sends for Jim, telling him he can have Tony if he can capture the horse.

Hervey warns Jordan away, telling the old man that Jim is gunning for him, and that Hervey will take care of everything. Meanwhile, Hervey and his crew raid Jordan's stock and blame the disappearances on Tony. But Jim figures out what's going on.

Jim captures Tony and manages to ride him until the saddle cinch breaks. The rider hits the ground, unconscious. Tony is tempted to stomp Jim just as he trampled Manuel, but he remembers that first caress. He sees Jim as a man to be trusted, "his new master!" He trails Jim to his line cabin after the man awakes.

There, Hervey ambushes the cowboy. Marianne overhears Hervey tell Jim that Jordan was the man who shot him. She gets the lowdown on the crooked ranch boss just as he's about to murder Jim. She runs him off, and Hervey leaves to clean out the stock from the Jordan ranch.

Jim and Marianne follow, and Tony follows them. But some of Hervey's men hang back to chase the

Marianne Jordan (Claire Adams) is aware of something that Red Ferris (Tom Mix) does not yet know. It was her father, Oliver Jordan, who years ago shot Red while he was playing his banjo.

hero and his gal. When they shoot Jim's horse out from under him, Tony arrives to carry him to safety. Then Jim and Marianne hurry to Jordan's hideaway, where Jim and Jordan bury the hatchet.

After affairs with Hervey are settled (off screen), Jim and Marianne lead Tony to the desert to release him. The horse wanders off, but returns to Jim. Marianne says, "He loves you more than—freedom!" Fade out.

The film differs from the novel in some ways, but captures the heart of the story—the untamed spirits of both Jim and Tony calling to one another. Most of Brand's novels contain more action or incident than would have fit into a movie of this sort; so some condensing for a film version works just fine. The romance between Jim and Marianne becomes a secondary issue; young viewers doubtless were far more interested in knowing whether their hero would survive Hervey's crooked scheming and end up with such a swell horse, than whether he got to kiss the girl. The filmic Jim sees Alcatraz/Tony first instead of Marianne. Hervey is perhaps more despicable in the movie, although he's more of a secondary character there than in the book. In the novel, Jim is shot while playing cards; in the film, he's playing an apparently obnoxious tune on a banjo.

What I find interesting is that the viewer never sees justice catch up to the bad guy, Hervey. Jim and Jordan shake hands and agree to fight no more, but no mention is made of Hervey after Tony rescues Jim. Odd. But I suppose providing thrills and chills was uppermost in the minds of the people making these movies; providing complete closure to all plot lines before the final reel ended was a secondary consideration. On the whole, though, *Just Tony* does good by the main concepts and action in Brand's novel, *Alcatraz*. ☐☐☐

TOM MIX IN "FLAMING GUNS"
and His NEW PONY, TONY, Jr.   A UNIVERSAL PICTURE

by Richard W. Bann

"So this is Lone Pine."

Raised in Mix Run, Pennsylvania, legendary showman and cowboy idol Thomas Edwin Mix (1880-1940) arose from humble beginnings. He later falsified his early bio until such time as his actual larger-than-life achievements and wealth outstripped any fantasy one could imagine. Contrary to studio biographies, the truth was that Mix left school after the fourth grade. He did serve as a Sergeant in the army during the Spanish-American War and other hostilities, but saw no battle action, and deserted the U.S. Artillery in 1902. At his funeral, however, director John Ford declared of Mix, "He was more loyal to his country and his friends than any man who ever lived." Always an expert marksman and horseman, Mix won a national rodeo championship in 1909. That same year, while working as a hunting guide and riding for a wild west show, Mix was engaged by the Selig Polyscope Company in Edendale, near Hollywood, as a wrangler and location scout for the latest thing in entertainment—motion pictures.

#14. Dewey Okla.
Tom Mix Bulldogging a Steer. Copyrighted by Drum & Griggs 7-12-10

Above: Tom Mix bulldogging a steer. This photo was taken on the Stokes Ranch in Dewey, Oklahoma on July 12, 1910, when Tom was first working in the movies.

Opposite page: Tom Mix about 1912 in Prescott, Arizona, where he played mostly supporting roles to Selig Polyscope star William Duncan. Tom's interest in fancy cowboy duds is already evident. The horse is "45," Tom Mix's first movie horse.

Below: Tom Mix and company at the Bachmann rental studio in Glendale, California, about 1914. Seated, left to right: cameraman Chuck Welty, Ed Brady, Victoria Forde, Eugenie Forde, Goldie Colwell, Tom Mix, unknown. On horseback, Pat Chrisman (fourth from right), "Dopey Dick" Crawford (third from right), Sid Jordan (extreme right).

It wasn't long before Mix was performing stunts and bit parts, then headlining Western short subjects he helped direct and produce for Selig from 1911 until 1917. That year he graduated to the Fox Film Corporation in a new series of short, comedic sagebrush adventures. Thereafter came the many exciting Fox feature films, aimed at the juvenile trade, which propelled the rising star above all other outdoor-action prairie pretenders, and secured his place in film history. With his distinctive sartorial splendor, atop "Tony, the Wonder Horse," Mix remained the reigning cowboy hero in movies until he retired (temporarily) with the arrival of talking pictures. More than that, in 1927 *Exhibitors Herald* polled theater owners and named Mix—not Chaplin, Chaney, Garbo, Pickford, Fairbanks, or Jolson—the number one box-office draw in America.

The much-imitated Mix himself controlled the folksy, escapist style of his formulaic films. He created the template followed by most subsequent celluloid cowboys. Nearly all the now familiar conventions and scenario-shorthand found in B Westerns into the 1950s can be traced to the Mix canon. Known for his colorful outfits, embroidered shirts, equestrian skills, and of course his celebrated mount, Tony, Mix invested both good-natured humor and action in his fanciful roles, performing a dazzling array of daredevil stunts. In so many of these hazardous scenes, it was unmistakably clear that Mix was risking his life. Forsaking the use of doubles, however, the athletic star sustained many serious injuries.

The Mix persona as a humble, clean-cut, All-American man of Prohibition Era virtue—like that of at least a dozen screen cowboys—was in sharp contrast to his real life of five wives, many affairs, alcohol, opulence, extravagance, and excess in several directions. His seven-car garage was crowded with expensive imports. As a titanic

Above: *Mr. Logan, U.S.A.* (Fox, 1918), Tom Mix and Kathleen Connors.

Right: *Prairie Trails* (Fox, 1920) Unknown and Tom Mix.

Above: *Do and Dare* (Fox, 1922)

Left: *The Lucky Horseshoe* (Fox, 1925) Tom Mix with frequent leading lady Billie Dove.

celebrity, he was photographed with endless royalty, dignitaries, and American presidents. In 1939, when the Tom Mix Circus was touring Europe, the headliner declined all engagements for Nazi Germany; Adolf Hitler himself phoned to extend his personal invitation. A neon sign atop the Mix mansion perpetually flashed his TM brand name into the sky. He made and spent fortunes. He lived large. He craved danger. One of his wives, Victoria Forde, actually shot him in 1924, and so admitted in court nine years later!

During his heyday, numerous Mix vehicles were adapted from best-selling novels by Zane Grey, one of which, *Riders of the Purple Sage* (1925), was lensed in Lone Pine. So was Mix's *Just Tony* (1922), based on the short story by Max Brand.

One of his concluding silent films was the aptly named *King Cowboy* (1928), as at that time there was no doubt this gun-toting immortal was King of all Cowboys. Years after his death, when Republic Pictures had labeled Roy Rogers the new King of the Cowboys, the Mix characterization still remained popular in comic books and on radio. There his voice was impersonated for another decade until 1950 in a program that began with the words, "The Tom Mix Ralston Six Shooters are on the air!"

Dale Evans, like many young ladies across America, dreamed of marrying Mix.

The influence, impact and enormous popularity of Tom Mix, from the mid-teens until his death in a speeding car crash on an Arizona highway in 1940, are long forgotten today. This is largely because he appeared in only nine talking feature films. Following another comeback made in a 1935 Mascot serial, some of these sound Universal features were reissued in 1936. There were only isolated revivals on

The second of five film versions of the famous Zane Grey novel, *Riders of the Purple Sage* (Fox, 1925).

television, however, and none has ever been licensed for cable television, videocassettes or DVDs.

Mix resisted talking pictures. For one thing, his gravel-processed voice betrayed "old" age. By 1932 the mileage on his 52 years was excessive, and was reflected in the clipped way he spoke. Mix was aware of this, was ever ill at ease near microphones, and had preferred to tour with John Ringling's Sells-Floto Circus than try talkies. Besides, there was a temporary decline in Westerns with the advent of sound in movies. But the stock market crash, bad investments, litigation with the IRS over accidental tax evasion, coupled with divorce, and child care maintenance, forced Mix to drag his bruised bones and artificially dyed jet-black hair back into the saddle.

Universal Pictures hoped to harness the Mix magic, so he signed to star in movies again. The contract called for six pictures the first season, and a follow-up arrangement promised six more for the second year (*Universal Weekly* stated it would be seven). The cowboy monarch was to be paid $30,000 per picture (that's more than the total negative cost on each of the six John Wayne Westerns Warner Bros. turned out for the 1932-33 season). The old warrior struggled mightily over two years to make it through only nine pictures, and then quit. He recommended the studio should re-sign Hoot Gibson to fill out their schedule, but he was under contract elsewhere and unavailable. That's how Ken Maynard was called back to Universal City, to succeed Mix.

At the outset, everyone wondered: Was Tom Mix still the undisputed "King of Western Stars!" as Universal's exploitation exclaimed? The initial five Mix vehicles, in particular the somber *Riders of Death Valley*, were outstanding series Westerns, and hold up as superior, class "A" entertainment today. Thereafter the decline was evident. Weathered, battered and scarred, Mix quickly discovered he was past the days of performing with ease those heralded, breathtaking stunts of yore. So the aging hero was increasingly doubled throughout the Universal series.

Dialogue, too, was a definite problem. Mix would slur his words, and pause, uncomfortably, in the middle of sentences. When John Wayne did so later, it was

One of the earliest Universal publicity shots of Tom Mix.

stylish. But Mix was plain awkward doing it, as if he'd forgotten the dialogue, was suddenly afraid, or didn't know what to say. Was it throat trouble? The story goes, according to Gene Autry, that Mix (his favorite actor, growing up) had long ago been shot in the jaw. At least there'd been an accident of some kind. "His false teeth troubled him constantly," Autry explained. "Every few sentences he would reach up and click those teeth back into place with his thumbs. His speech was what you call deliberate." The voice did not reflect the comic flair which audiences could only suppose from the silent Fox adventures, and which they expected in talkies.

The inaugural entry for the second season of six (or seven) was slated to be *Flaming Guns*. Announced as a remake of the 1926 well-received Hoot Gibson vehicle, *The Buckaroo Kid*, the property was based on a short story "Oh, Promise Me," which Peter B. Kyne wrote for *Collier's* magazine. This also served as the working title for a while. Actually the project had been slated for Mix much earlier, then shelved, then officially postponed as of an April 5, 1932 item in the show biz bible, *Variety*. By late summer, however, the yarn was revived for pre-production work to kick off the 1932-33 campaign. The trade paper *Hollywood Filmograph* carried a story in its September 17, 1932 issue that began, "Tom Mix is celebrating his 24th season on the screen with the starting of his second consecutive Universal contract. The cowboy star has been active in motion pictures longer than any other cinema actor."

Assigned to steer the show was the only director who served on more than one of the nine Universal films, Art Rosson. He directed two, and was uncredited for work on others. Rosson was then less than a year away from becoming Jean Harlow's brother-in-law.

She married Hal Rosson, a distinguished British-born cinematographer at M-G-M, with credits including *The Wizard of Oz* (1939) and *Singing in the Rain* (1952). Brother Art's resumé included silent Westerns with Mix, and several with Hoot Gibson, including a pair lensed on location in Lone Pine: *Points West* (1929), and *Trailin' Trouble* (1930). Later, Rosson had a long association with Cecil B. De Mille as a second unit director, and functioned in that capacity shooting action scenes on several other big films, including *Gone with the Wind* (1939) and *Red River* (1948). Ironic, then, that *Flaming Guns*, especially with its exciting title, is often criticized for its paucity of drama and thrills. In fairness, this comedy-edged entry is more in keeping with the silent era Mix vehicles—a blend of lighthearted action and stunts.

Being a retread of a Hoot Gibson tongue-in-cheek horse opera accounts for this entry as the lone Universal subject played primarily for laughs. The prolific Jack Cunningham wrote the adaptation, and served as scenarist on four of the other Mix Universals. Cunningham needs no more praise for his work than to mention he crafted screenplays on the best W.C. Fields comedies at Paramount.

Mix's regular cinematographer, Dan Clark, who shot all the other Universals, was on loan to M-G-M for a special assignment in Alaska. Behind the lens in his place was Jerry Ash, earning his only Lone Pine credit. Judging the merits of his cinematography up in the Alabama Hills framed by Lone Pine's lush mountain landscape is quite naturally compounded by the multitude of spectacular views afforded by any camera

Still photo issued with *Flaming Guns*. There is just such a scene in the film (and in many Mix films), but it was not shot exactly here. Plus, Mix wears that vest in several of his Universal films, but not in *Flaming Guns*. Note the LP designation in the background mountain landscape, there to let airplane pilots know they are flying over Lone Pine. Usually, movie-makers would pay local kids to cover the sign so they could shoot there.

set-up there, pointing in any direction, at any time of day. Those automatic and prodigious production values inherent in all scenic exterior sequences are the reasons crews were so often attracted to Lone Pine in the first place. Midway through *Flaming Guns* there is a sweeping, cattle rustling sequence out in the rocks that is especially stirring, scored as it was with pulse-pounding cues to be used again so effectively throughout the same studio's 1936 chapter play *The Phantom Rider*, starring Buck Jones, the same actor Fox had hired a decade previously as star insurance to keep Tom Mix in line.

Universal was well known for nepotism and, as the series progressed, Mix resented interference from so many of studio founder Carl Laemmle's kin, calling them "a lot of supervisors and yes-men and assistant yes-men with more red tape than an Indian agent." Having long bossed his own unit, Mix wasn't used to working that way. Their disputes were covered in the Hollywood trade papers and, according to an item in *Variety* on October 4, Mix insisted that all Laemmle relatives be removed from supervisory and direction posts on his productions. The story has created

some confusion for Mix filmographers, because it also stated, "Henry MacRae will direct the next Mix feature, which will not be "Oh, Promise Me," which has been moved back so that a yarn with more hair on its chest can be substituted."

First, "Oh, Promise Me" (which coincidentally was also the title of an unrelated stage show Universal owned, and had announced for the screen in 1931, but shelved in 1932) would be renamed with action in mind as *Flaming Guns*. The new title was conferred after principal photography and location shooting in Lone Pine, which took place throughout October. The new designation was an improvement, but misleading, since the "flaming guns" in question were shown and heard only during a few seconds of opening overseas World War I stock footage—from Universal's own *All Quiet on the Western Front* (1930).

Then, according to the November 19 issue of *Hollywood Filmograph*, the subsequent Henry MacRae project for Mix, *Terror Trail* (which MacRae would supervise, but Armand Schaefer would direct), "started Monday at Lone Pine, California."

Universal director and serial supervisor Henry McRae visits Tom Mix and William Farnum on the sets of *Flaming Guns* (Universal, 1933). Although Tom Mix signed for a second series of six Westerns for Universal for the 1933-1934 season, nagging injuries from his movie stunts led Mix to walk away from this contract after three films.

So *Flaming Guns* was shot before *Terror Trail*. Also, the respective release dates for *Flaming Guns* of December 22, and for *Terror Trail* on the following February 2, were never changed, as reflected by the charts in all available trade papers throughout their listings for months. There was, however, a delay in granting booking dates for prints on this seventh (not eighth) of nine Mix Universals, *Flaming Guns*. That left the eighth entry being *Terror Trail*, and *Rustlers Roundup* concluding the series.

In the November 19 issue of *Universal Weekly*, the studio announced the retirement of Mix's faithful steed, Tony, to a stable in the nearby green hills of Universal City. In his place, seven year-old Tony, Jr., a chestnut sorrel of mixed blood, and a few shades darker, but with similar markings, was designated to

Mix with a supposed "Tony," and daughter Thomasina. Note the cane used while recovering from a costly spill that spelled the difference between profit and loss on the production.

make his debut in *Flaming Guns*. "He was given to me," Mix explained, "by an admiring friend about four years ago because he so closely resembles great old Tony. I've been working with him ever since because of his intelligence and willingness to work. He has worked in scenes before, and Tony, Sr. has coached him, too."

In fact, Tony, Jr. had worked in all the sound era "scenes before." Tony, Sr. had been retired since 1929, well before the Universal series. The quickest way to differentiate the two, unless their doubles are involved, just as Ken Maynard's Tarzan and Roy Rogers' Trigger, also utilized multiple lookalike understudies and stand-ins, was that Tony carried white stockings on only his hind legs, while Tony, Jr. had four white stockings. Incidentally, one of Tony, Jr.'s doubles was acquired by Gene Autry in 1938, to serve as one of his horse Champion's doubles, primarily performing as Autry's touring horse.

Why so much fabrication surrounding Tom Mix? Perhaps more than any other Hollywood celebrity? First, Mix, himself, encouraged it, to build and perpetuate his legend. Second, these were movies, not documentaries, and Hollywood was selling illusions and dreams, not reporting news. More importantly, the Mix market, according to his own estimation, was 60% kids. They were vulnerable, impressionable, and easy to fool with the appealing unreality being offered. Especially during Mix's time, when America was a different place.

The same November 19 *Universal Weekly* story also mentioned how Tony, Jr. "stumbled in jumping a fence and fell on his rider crushing two of his ribs." An Associated Press still photo, datelined October 21, confirmed as much and stated that the horse "tripped and fell upon (Mix) in the filming of a thrilling scene at Lone Pine, Calif. Several hours after the accident Mix was still unconscious." The photograph showed a recovering Mix holding a cane, standing next to his nine year-old daughter, Thomasina, astride Tony, Jr. Mix suffered severe internal injuries, and the accident delayed completing the film. *Flaming Guns* was budgeted for 15 days during October, but now would take 22. This constituted a material overrun and an important setback for the production.

Locations included not only the Alabama Hills west of Lone Pine, but also Big Pine, Bridgeport, Mojave, Red Rock Canyon State Park, and the Brandt Rancho

On location in the rock-studded Alabama Hills, rounding up rustlers in *Flaming Guns*.

Flaming Guns photo posed for the camera, not reflecting the film's action. Mix has just been arrested and told William Farnum that the next time they meet, "I'm going to split your ears."

near Girard, all in California. Shooting afforded a variety of Lone Pine views: Mount Whitney, the Sierras, the Alabama Hills, the town itself, and what appears to be Whitney Portal Road—then only a dirt road.

Mix's contract gave him approval over all casting decisions. On November 8 (with filming concluded), *Variety* carried this item: "William Farnum, who preceded Tom Mix as Fox's big money Western star in the old days, is in a supporting part in Mix's 'Oh, Promise Me.'" He was the brother of actor Dustin Farnum (for whom Dustin Hoffman was named), but not Franklyn Farnum. He starred in the original 1918 adaptation of *Riders of the Purple Sage*, remade by Mix, as mentioned, in Lone Pine. Nor was this the sole instance of a screen role Farnum created, only to be reduced to a character part in the remake years later. *The Lone Star Ranger, The Last of the Duanes,*

If I Were King, The Spoilers, and *Samson* are some examples.

Farnum was 56 in *Flaming Guns*, looked older, and needed to, since Mix was 52. With his usual line of snappy patter, "Windy Bill" tended to chew the scenery pretty good, and few directors were able to tone down his grand, theatrical style of acting. With those up-and-down, ever-animated bushy eyebrows, it always seemed that Farnum could have inspired the *Howdy Doody Show* character on early television, Mr. Bluster. Yet somehow his scene-stealing histrionics in a comedic Western like *Flaming Guns* served the role well. One wonders if the verbal sparring between Mix and the ornery Farnum throughout the film was animated by their real-life, past competition for supremacy at Fox, extending back to the early 1920s. In the teens, Farnum was publicized as the single highest paid cinema star. He lost a fortune in the

Wall Street crash, however, and filed a petition for bankruptcy while *Flaming Guns* was still playing in movie theaters.

Cast to portray J. P. Mulford—and uncharacteristically sympathetic here—was that hatchet-faced, miserly meanie, Clarence H. Wilson. Clarence E. Mulford was the celebrated author of the Hopalong Cassidy yarns. Seeing *Flaming Guns* today, one might suspect the Mix unit was poking fun at the Hoppy series. Except that in 1932, no Hopalong Cassidy Westerns had yet been made! The only screen adaptation to date of any Mulford literary property had been his *The Orphan*, first in 1920 as the same-named film starring William Farnum, and then four years later as *The Deadwood Coach*, starring who else but Tom Mix. Mulford and Mix were friendly enough to exchange Christmas cards.

The Mix Universals were more than special B Westerns, and with some racy dialogue and scenes, this one leaves no doubt it was made as a pre-Code picture, too. Ingénue Ruth Hall was engaged as Farnum's disobedient daughter. At 21, this raven-haired beauty was 31 years younger than Mix. She spins her role as quite a liberated young lady. They made an interesting couple, since neither appeared entirely comfortable delivering dialogue.

As a society debutante from Florida, films had appealed to Miss Hall. Her uncle was Vicente Blasco Ibanez, author of *The Four Horsemen of the Apocalypse*, the screen vehicle for Rudolph Valentino. She parlayed her looks into status as a 1932 class Wampas Baby Star (with Ginger Rogers), regular high-end parties at Pickfair and San Simeon, and roles with the Marx Brothers in *Monkey Business* (1931), and *The Kid From Spain* (1932) with Eddie Cantor. In Westerns she made two with John Wayne plus a serial, and was Ken Maynard's favorite leading lady in three of his best films.

Before she married and lived happily ever after with distinguished, Oscar-winning cinematographer Lee Garmes (who coincidentally had worked on the 1921 Valentino picture), he pursued her ardently, sending limousines to studios and locations to pick her up when shooting would finish each day.

In person, later in life, Ruth Hall was warm and gracious. She remembered what a "gentleman Tom Mix was. He was a gentleman," she recalled in 1977, "and he played more of a gentleman than a cowboy

Ruth Hall portrait issued for *Flaming Guns*.

in our picture. I met him for the first time, and within minutes we were shooting our first scene together. We hardly rehearsed anything. It was a pleasure. He was wonderful, he looked out for me, whereas the director paid little attention to anything I was doing. It was the same in all the Westerns I did; nobody gave me any direction. It seemed Tom was actually in charge, making so many decisions, blocking out scenes, and so forth. He knew what everyone else should be doing, and helped them, too. He knew his lines, he knew my lines, and we got many scenes right on the first take. I had to do my own make-up and hair, and when you work outside in the middle of the day, it's so easy to get sun burnt, which I usually did! But no one seemed to care about 'the girl,' or pay any attention, except

Tom. Still, he was reserved. Polite, but reserved. He made everything easy. I liked him."

In a signature Lone Pine scene, Miss Hall and her two presumed sisters are riding in the back of Farnum's open roadster as it passes through town from the south side. Stopping at the now long-gone Gilmore Gasoline Rainbow Station, framed by the majestic Mount Whitney and adjacent, snow-capped Sierra Nevada Mountains in the background to the west, one of the young ladies is moved to exclaim, "So this is Lone Pine!"

"Yes, isn't it gorgeous?" adds Hall. "I've always been crazy about the country up here."

Her sister asks, "Where are the pines?"

Farnum answers, trying to be funny, "Just pined away."

Mix was known to monogram his clothes and manifold possessions. The distinctive TM-bar logo on the hubcaps betrays that the magnificent Rolls Royce that Farnum was driving in fact belonged to the film's star. Mix must have driven it up to Lone Pine himself, doubtless violating all posted speed limits, typically racing to his destination as always.

Also in the show: familiar favorites Eddie Baker, Pee Wee Holmes, Fred Burns, Slim Whitaker, Bud Osborne and, beginning his steep ascension towards becoming the first actor in Hollywood ever to win three Academy Awards, Walter Brennan. He won

Tom Mix as Sergeant Tom Malone returns home, driven by his Army chauffeur, played by Clyde Kinney in this early scene from *Flaming Guns*. Partially shown is the roadside guidepost greeting them as they near the town of Lone Pine. At the bottom of this sign, the elevation for Mount Whitney is given as 14,497 feet. In *High Sierra* (1940), Humphrey Bogart is informed by gas station attendant Spencer Charters that the sawtoothed peak's elevation is 14,501. In the remake, *I Died A Thousand Times* (1955), gas station attendant Dub Taylor tells Jack Palance that the highest point in the United States and the pride of the Sierras is 14,496 feet above sea level. The true, exact elevation remains in contention.

his third Oscar for *The Westerner* with Gary Cooper, released in the fall of 1940 and playing in movie theaters when Tom Mix raced—ever racing—to his death, perishing on a highway. It was the same year that old friend John Ford, then in the midst of shooting *The Grapes of Wrath*, met with Mix at Fox and was saddened to tell the star whose hit movies built the studio that there was no place for him there, "This picture business has passed you by a long time ago." Ford remembered walking the depressed icon back to the gate. Times were changing, again.

The story: Tom Mix plays a veteran of The Great War who in 1918 returns, in uniform, to the town of Lone Pine. He passes a sign that reads, "1 Mile to Lone Pine. Gateway to Mount Whitney. Highest peak in the United States. Elevation 14,497 feet." There he is greeted and re-hired by rancher Clarence Wilson to combat cattle rustlers. Later, city banker William Farnum, also a rancher, and a friendly rival of Wilson, learns of Mix's success in this venture, and lures him away to become foreman of Farnum's Rancho Casa Grande. Cattle have been mysteriously disappearing from the spread during the crooked stewardship of Duke Lee. Mix rides to Farnum's ranch and, in negotiating his remuneration, asks for 25% of all profits. He also asks Farnum's daughter, Ruth Hall, to lunch.

Increasingly at odds with Mix over his perceived impudence, and his interest in daughter Hall, the blustery Farnum tries to fire him. Farnum departs for the city, but Mix defies his boss. Possessing a written letter of authority, Mix remains in charge at the ranch, while romancing Hall. Later, upon learning that Mix has not departed, the infuriated Farnum

Cantankerous old friends Clarence H. Wilson and William Farnum arguing, to the amusement of Ruth Hall. October shooting in Lone Pine was chilly enough for coats and gloves.

Tom Mix, as Tom Malone, arrives at the office of William Farnum, as Henry Ramsey, for an appointment about a job in this scene from *Flaming Guns*.

MR. RAMSEY

PRIVATE

Ruth Hall and Tom Mix all set for some Prohibition-era fun at the Tip-Top Club in this scene from *Flaming Guns*.

Tom Mix asks Ruth Hall to lunch. Their relative ages were not discussed during *Flaming Guns*, but he was 52, and she was 21. William Farnum, as her cantankerous father, objected to virtually everything about Mix, except his age. Farnum was 56.

rushes back to his property—only to discover Mix in the process of apprehending the old foreman, Lee, plus his gang of varmints, and thwarting more cattle rustling. But Farnum misunderstands, and refuses to listen as his daughter defends Mix. Then the irate father has Mix arrested for trespassing.

In the course of time Farnum relents, and tries to rescind the complaint, but only upon condition that Mix leaves the territory and will never see Farnum's daughter again. While this discussion is going on, Mix escapes jail, and invokes a playful threat made earlier—that he would split Farnum's ears if ever he failed to give Mix what he asked for. Now Farnum is petrified at such news, and sends word that he offers Mix his job back, plus 50% interest in all profits.

Mix rides to the ranch, secretly meets with Hall, and says he wants 100% interest in *her*. They flee on horseback to cross the border and marry in Mexico,

with Farnum racing after them in hot pursuit by auto, believing his daughter has been kidnapped. The Mexican immigration authorities, evidently operating under a different mandate than they have today, easily allow Mix to pass, and acquiesce to block Farnum when he tries to cross the border!

The domestic release date for this seventh of nine Mix Universals was December 22. But trade screenings were delayed until June of 1933. *Film Daily* hailed *Flaming Guns* as "a very good Western with plenty of good comedy predominating in the story. This one is way ahead of most Westerns. A good story, well acted and directed. Good fun for everyone."

The critic for *Motion Picture Daily* reported, "This is one of the best Tom Mix Westerns in a long time. It is set in a modern after-the-war background, with some city sequences, and a good story. In addition,

Near the *Flaming Guns* finish line, passport problems for William Farnum at the border seem to amuse Clarence H. Wilson. The key reveal in this still photo cannot be discovered by watching the film. Throughout the picture, Farnum is presented as the rich banker-rancher who owns this magnificent Rolls Royce (off-screen, he would soon declare bankruptcy). In fact, the hubcap emblazoned with the distinctive "TM" brand indicates the auto belonged to the film's star and that Tom Mix drove it to Lone Pine!

comedy is sprinkled all the way through it. A Tivoli (Theatre) audience chuckled and guffawed and made other signs of approval. Most of the outdoor scenery is laid in the Owens Valley section of California around Lone Pine, with the magnificent mountains in the background."

The picture hides a quick throwaway scene, easy to miss, written by Jack Cunningham. Of all people, depraved-looking Jim Corey, denizen of rock bottom independent Westerns made for less than the cost of Mix's wardrobe (though he does wear a tuxedo during the roadhouse raid), has a surprising pre-Code dialogue exchange. While riding along next to another cowpoke while herding some cattle, he asks, "Where'd you say you was born?" The other cowpuncher responds, "I was born out of wedlock."

Corey chimes in, "That's a mighty funny country up there."

In a regular feature, *The Motion Picture Herald* offered exhibitors a forum to share random thoughts on how well any given picture played, and what kind of business it generated. The blunt, unvarnished contributions were always of interest. Some frank assessments of *Flaming Guns* from theater managers all over America in 1933:

"Drew average Saturday night business, and pleased."

"One of the best Westerns we ever played with Tom Mix."

"Fine, different type of Western. Pleased majority."

"Tom Mix at his best. Will more than please Mix

fans and general patronage on Saturdays. Plenty of action and cleverly done throughout."

"For the first time in months we had them standing with this. Mix still gives them a fast performance despite his age."

"Personally, think this the best picture Tom Mix ever made. No unnecessary shooting, he did not fight half-dozen men single-handed, the heroine was fine."

Taglines to promote the picture included these:

"Tom Mix and his NEW pony, Tony, Jr."

"A smashing, crashing, dashing picture presenting a Peter B. Kyne story of red courage and sizzling action in the Mt. Whitney cow country!"

"Flaming guns, cattle stampedes, and one of the greatest manhunts in history, with the glorious Mt. Whitney cow-country as a gorgeous background!"

According to the studio press book, exhibitors could purchase six "personality stills" for fifty cents, in total, at "your local Universal exchange." Admission, at even the downtown movie palaces around the country, averaged less than that small sum of nickels and dimes. And what sum would collectors pay for those period original still photos today?

Results at the box-office did not disappoint:

Domestic film rental: $120,391.38

Foreign revenue: $66,977.06

Worldwide total: $187,368.44.

Those were big numbers in the 1930s, and in assessing profit and loss figures vis-à-vis film grosses today, one needs to be cognizant of inflation and the incredible price level changes that have taken place over time.

The problem with *Flaming Guns* was a budget overrun, resulting in an excessive cost of $103,135.60. The subsequent entry in the series, *Terror Trail*, also shot in Lone Pine, had a negative cost of only $89,482.72. It grossed less, yet still turned a profit. Whereas *Flaming Guns* lost $5,687.26.

Two days before the scheduled release date of December 22, a story in *Variety* declared that Tom Mix and Universal were dissolving their relationship by mutual agreement: "Mix says recent accidents and influenza convinced him he needs a rest.... He has suffered 26 broken bones and many wounds while in production."

The New York Times announced simultaneously,

The big Western star, riding to the rescue of all your fans who are fed up on drawing room dramas and pink-tea heroes. Coming Soon in 'FLAMING GUNS'

"He will quit on Christmas Day after completion of his latest picture, *Rustlers Roundup*."

Mix told boss Carl Laemmle, "I've nearly died twice makin' these films. The risks aren't worth it anymore."

When Ken Maynard replaced Tom Mix as Universal's Western star, profits soared, because costs were held in check. The expensive seven-day shooting delay in the schedule, caused by Mix's accident, plus his own excessive salary, shot down *Flaming Guns*. It meant the difference between profit and loss, success and failure. Time was running out for Tom Mix ... though still ever racing, as fast as he could. There would be the serial, *The Miracle Rider*, then worldwide touring, the circus, but no more feature films.

Two days short of exactly two years after Mix died, on October 12, 1940, *The New York Times* reported Tony's passing, in his stall at age 32 on October 10, 1942.

In 1947, a stone monument, topped by the metal horse cutout depicting a riderless Tony, was dedicated to the memory of Tom Mix at the exact

Scene from *Terror Trail*, made in Lone Pine's tumbled terrain immediately following *Flaming Guns*.

spot on the lonely Arizona highway where he lost his life. Gene Autry presided at the ceremony. Today it remains a tourist attraction as part of a highway rest stop.

In 2011, a retired Arizona businessman, Bob White, completed a restoration of the 1937 Cord 812 Phaeton classic auto Mix died in. White paid $240,000 for the car. He spent more than that renovating it. As a barometer for better understanding the comparative P&L numbers on *Flaming Guns* in today's dollars, the way one would, if using discounted present value calculations, Mix's Cord sold new, in 1937, for the total price of $2,700.

Tom Mix lived large indeed. It remains a sad commentary that today so few remember the man who was cinema's foremost cowboy star.

Biographer Paul Mix wrote of his relative, "He did his best to publicly represent those virtues which at one time were respected by most Americans."

Universal preserved its nitrate preprint elements on *Flaming Guns* in the mid-1990s, but the one 35mm exhibition print they made went up in "flames" in a news-making vault fire on the lot in 2008. Fortunately, the negative and fine grain preprint materials were stored elsewhere in the studio's principal film archive. Assurances from Universal are that they will strike a new circulating print, costing approximately $5,000, by year's end. ☐☐☐

THE LAST RIDE OF
TOM MIX

by Gary Eugene Brown

He rode the open range
Across the silver screen
Down sawdust trails thru purple sage
And in a young man's dreams
Dreams don't last forever
But the memories never die
Out there, West of Yesterday,
Where Tom Mix will always ride

—Don Edwards, *"West of Yesterday"*

America's first King of the Cowboys, the "Idol of a Million Boys," Tom Mix was headed north on the highway from Tucson to Phoenix on October 12, 1940. He was driving a pale yellow, customized, 1937 Cord convertible with the top down. Tom was wearing a crème-colored Western-style suit, custom-made hat, boots, and a belt with a silver belt buckle that had his name embossed on it with a large diamond encased in the center. He intended on stopping just up the road in Florence to see his former son-in-law, rodeo champion Harry Knight, who had been married to his eldest daughter Ruth. Tom stopped at Oracle Junction for a quick bite to eat, visited with some of the folks there, and got back on the road.

The time was approximately 2:15 PM. Driving in the middle of nowhere in the Arizona desert, Tom felt like it was alright to open up his turbo charged Cord because, after all, it was built to be driven fast. Suddenly, he saw a road crew working on a bridge embankment near one of the many dry washes that traverse the highway. In the split of a second, realizing that he'd most likely run over the workers, he braked hard and jerked the steering wheel, flipping his automobile. The Cord ended upside down, with the wheels still spinning. State highway worker John Adams, from Oracle, who had tried to flag the car down when he heard the roar of the powerful engine, went running to the overturned vehicle with co-worker E.A. Armeta of Casa Grande, turned over the Cord, and found Tom Mix unconscious, in repose as if taking a nap, without a mark on him. However, the cowboy hero of the silver screen who had survived many dangerous stunts in his lengthy film career was not able to recover this time. It is surmised a metal suitcase behind the front seat became airborne and struck Tom, breaking his neck. The King is dead . . . long live the new King!

Tom Mix had lived a charmed life up to that fateful day. He was 60 years old and, contrary to Hollywood legend, had not been born astride a horse in El Paso, Texas. He was never a Texas Ranger, nor did he fight in the Mexican Revolution. However, he did lead a most interesting life that needed very little embellishing. Born the son of a teamster in Mix Run, Pennsylvania, he very early learned his way around horses, but not so much around women, as he eventually married five times. Tom went west to Oklahoma where he became a hired hand with the Miller Brothers 101 Ranch and Wild West Show. With a natural gift of gab, a winsome personality and classic good looks, he was able to secure an acting position with the Selig Polyscope Film Company, who often filmed at the 101 Ranch. Tom went on to make numerous one and two reel silent films from 1909 to 1918 for Selig.

Tom then signed with Fox Studios. William Fox, the former haberdasher, now movie mogul, made him an international film star and Tom eventually became the highest paid actor in Hollywood. As an aside, the films of Tom Mix made the money at the box office that allowed Fox to produce less popular genres of films (dramas and romantic comedies), literally carrying Fox Studios during its early years. A contract dispute in 1928 ended the partnership that had lasted a decade. Tom soon signed with political patriarch Joseph Kennedy's FBO Studios and continued to make silent Western films even though the "talkies" were the current rage. Studios were quickly changing over to produce only sound films. Sadly, the FBO films were not of the same

He rode the open range
Across the silver screen
Down sawdust trails thru purple sage
And in a young man's dreams
Dreams don't last forever
But the memories never die
Out there, West of Yesterday,
Where Tom Mix will always ride
—Don Edwards

quality as the Fox films and the last Tom Mix silent film was released in November 1928.

The Wall Street Crash of 1929 and a testy divorce struck Tom particularly hard as he lost approximately one million dollars in the stock market, his Beverly Hills mansion, and his ranch in Arizona. However, being the consummate showman, Tom remade himself and hit the sawdust trail with the Sells-Floto Circus as their featured main act, for which he was paid a whopping $20,000 per week. Truth be told, Tom loved performing before his adoring fans and preferred it to making photoplays where there was no interaction with the audience.

However, Carl Laemmle, co-founder of Universal Studios, thought the former cowboy megastar could easily make the transition to sound movies and signed him to make nine Western films beginning in 1932. Tom, at age 52, could still ride like the wind and perform most of his own stunts.

The Ralston Purina Company, like Universal, thought the name Tom Mix still had a significant drawing power and negotiated a deal with him to bring *The Tom Mix Ralston Straight Shooters* radio program to NBC in September 1933. The 15-minute, three-times-a-week, adventure series ran for an unbelievable twenty years, ten on NBC and ten on the Mutual network. It, along with *Jack Armstrong, The All-American Boy*, a similarly formatted juvenile adventure program with a nearly identical broadcast history, defined an era; they opened and closed it. The Mix show was one of the great premium givers, flooding the mails with decoders, whistling badges, photo albums, comics and similar items. The price was a dime and one or two box tops. However, Tom Mix never portrayed himself on the popular program and had nothing to do with it beyond lending his name. The show was so popular it lasted for nearly 15 years past his death.

After his contract with Universal expired, Tom,

still enchanted by the circus life, was able to buy the Sam B. Dill Circus in 1934. It was renamed the Tom Mix Circus and he began the annual circuit tour around the country. Tom soon realized that operating a circus, with its many employees, animals and rolling stock, required considerable capital.

Film producer Nat Levine came along at a time beneficial to both he and Tom. He signed Tom to star in a 15-chapter serial—*The Miracle Rider*—for his Mascot Films. Tom was only required to spend one month filming the cliffhanger for his salary of $40,000. No expense was spared as *The Miracle Rider* was given a sizeable budget for the time ($80,000) and it paid off handsomely as the serial grossed over one million dollars for Mascot, the most ever from their many serials. Sadly, this was to be Tom Mix's last film.

Tom continued to run and appear with the Tom Mix Circus up until 1938. Rising costs and increased competition took its toll on Tom. As a result, during this period, he began to drink heavily. Almost destitute, he left the circus in the hands of his daughter Ruth while he went to Europe hoping to make money with a vaudeville act. The circus soon folded and was sold off to help settle its debts. Tom, meanwhile, received a wonderful reception in the United Kingdom and Scandinavia. It motivated him to think about returning to making Western films and perhaps even form another wild west show.

Tom, still looking younger than he really was, decided he would visit Fox Studios, now 20th Century Fox, to determine if there was any possibility he might be given a chance to once again make Western films for the studio he had helped put on the map. The studio's Production Manager Lefty Hough arranged for Tom to meet with the renowned director John Ford who was then filming *The Grapes of Wrath*. Ford, who had been the director of a few Tom Mix films, took Tom out to lunch and enjoyed catching up but, the truth be told, there was no interest in the studio featuring yesteryear's cowboy film hero.

Tom's last journey began in New York, driving west in his customized 1937 Cord. He went to Chicago before heading to the Southwest, where he stopped by the historic King Ranch for a brief visit and then headed west to El Paso. He stayed at a dude ranch north of the city to visit Slim Harris, a former horse trainer. There he met Gene Sterling, who had been

Above: Tom Mix, circa 1910.

Below: Tom, circa 1924.

a child actor in several of Tom's early films. The 17-year-old actor and artist was working in the office at the guest ranch while doubling as an entertainer. Sterling asked Tom if he could hitch a ride to Las Cruces, New Mexico, to pick up a saddle he had left for repair. Tom agreed and Sterling helped load a couple of metal suitcases into the Cord. Sterling, riding shotgun, recalled that on the open highway Tom opened it up and the speedometer topped out at one point. The manufacturer noted the top speed for the turbocharged version of the 1937 Cord was 150 mph!

After dropping off Sterling, Tom went on to Lordsburg, New Mexico, known to Western-film enthusiasts as the final destination of the Ringo Kid in the classic film *Stagecoach*. Lordsburg was a thriving town in October 1940, and a popular stop for motorists between El Paso and Tucson. Tom had accepted an invitation to be the Grand Marshal in their annual Fair Day Parade and was provided a blue roan named Smokey to ride. It was Smokey's first parade, and turned out to be the last ride on horseback for the famous cowboy hero and Tom's farewell parade before an adoring crowd.

After visiting an old friend, Blackie Baugh, in Lordsburg, Tom fired up the Cord and headed west to Old Tucson where he checked into the historic Santa Rita Hotel. Tom called his old friend Sheriff Ed Echols to arrange a social get together. In turn, Sheriff Echols called his friend Walt Coburn, a popular western author of the day, and left a message with Walt's wife that he was bringing Tom Mix over for a drink later that afternoon. The day was October 11, 1940.

Tom and Ed went to Walt's ranch where they proceeded to roll their smokes and drink whiskey. They swapped stories about the time when both Tom and the Sheriff were with the Miller Brothers 101 Ranch and Wild West Show. The evening concluded with the three old amigos watching the sun set in the west. It would be Tom's last sunset.

Before leaving the Coburn ranch, Tom gave Walt an autographed copy of his book *Roping a Million*. They agreed to come back the next day for a bar-b-que and Ed Echols drove Tom back to his hotel. Tom decided to have a drink in the hotel bar and listened to the house band under the direction of Maurice Carl. He invited the band up to his room for drinks and a party commenced carrying into the wee hours of the morning. Tom supposedly told them "buenas noches" at about 3:00 AM, as he had to get up to drive north to Phoenix. Some people believe that Tom's youngest daughter Thomasina was residing in Phoenix and had recently given birth and he wanted to see his new grandchild.

Ed Echols ran into Tom at the hotel the next day and Tom told him that he was going to forgo the invite to the Coburn Ranch so he could head north. He checked out of the hotel at noon and visited briefly with the hotel manager Nick Hall and Tucson motor officer Dick Lease. Officer Lease gave Tom directions to Florence and Phoenix.

Later, Officer Lease heard a report that there had been an accident involving a Cord roadster on Highway 89, so he proceeded to the scene knowing it had to have involved Tom Mix. Nick Hall at the Santa Rita heard about the accident and notified Sheriff Ed Echols, who also responded to the scene. Hall in turn phoned Tom's daughters Ruth and Thomasina as to what he had heard about the fate of their father. When Walt Coburn heard the news he just saddled up and rode off into the desert to collect his thoughts. An ambulance and the coroner were dispatched to the scene. Coroner E.O. Divine later said the legendary cowboy star had been killed instantly and that there would be no inquest.

> *I remember his last sun down*
> *As he watched that crimson desert sky*
> *Do you think he knew the morning dove*
> *were singing their last good bye*
> *Do you think he chose this place to die*
> *Did he plan his destiny*
> *The answers in the desert wind*
> *Where his spirit still rides free*
> —Don Edwards

Tom Mix and Dorothy Dwan photographed on one of Tom's many roadsters in 1929 to help publicize the FBO film *The Drifter*.

Well-known stunt pilot Paul Mantz flew Tom's wife Mable Ward Mix and a friend to Florence to claim the body. The Cord, not heavily damaged, was towed to a garage in Florence. A number of friends were at the Union Air Terminal when Mantz's plane took off for the return to Los Angeles with Tom's remains.

Upon hearing the tragic news of Tom Mix's death, William S. Hart, cowboy film star and close friend of Tom's, remarked, "It's just too awful. My recollections of Tom are still very vivid. He was wonderful." Tom's body was kept at the Pierce Brothers Mortuary.

Friends and fans alike paid their respects at the Little Church of Flowers. Actor and close friend Monte Blue read a Masonic ritual. Reverend J. Whitcomb Bougher oversaw the services. Tom received full Masonic and military honors, the latter thanks to John Ford, as Tom had deserted his second tour of duty to be with his wife. No one said no to John Ford.

Pallbearers were LA County Sheriff Eugene Biscailuz, John Ford, Monte Blue, B. Reeves Easton, Col. Monte Stone, Howard Nowlin, Dan Clark (Tom's cameraman at Fox) and his attorney Ivon D. Parker. Those attending the service included

OCTOBER 13, 1940.

U. S. URGED
MBUS FETE

Tom Mix, Rider of Circus and Films, Killed When His Auto Overturns on Arizona Road

DIETERICH
FORMER S

ing Anniversary
ry of America
d for Faith

ENS PRAISED

ssage Sent to
ails Loyalty
or Speak

ary of the dis-
was made the
y speakers at
rations for a
the essential
of all racial
ation of con-

background
and threats
mocracy, of-
ders stressed
usual, the
place in Co-
about 10,000
ov. Charles
President
whispering
ell Willkie

Continued From Page One

films he rode a horse named Tony. The magnificent animal developed a following of its own that won companion billing on theatre marquees with its master. Tony was retired in November, 1932, at the age of 23, in the Mix stables in Universal City.

The official biography of Mr. Mix had him born in Texas but that was evidently for publicity purposes. His Pennsylvania birthplace has been verified.

In 1898 he joined the Army and saw service in Cuba as one of Colonel Theodore Roosevelt's Rough Riders, and later he saw service with the American troops in the Philippines.

When the Boxer rebellion broke out in China Mr. Mix went there with the American forces. For distinguished service in the Orient he received a medal and a citation. He also did a turn as a soldier of fortune, going to South Africa and fighting with the British in the Boer War, taking part in the siege of Ladysmith.

Crack Shot Peace Officer

The Army did not sate his taste for adventure and, on returning to the United States, he became a law enforcement officer in Kansas, Oklahoma and Texas, where, even at that late day, there

Tom Mix

sponsibility. He could never smoke a cigarette in a picture, nor could he enter a saloon except to deal justice to a "bad man."

His movie love affairs were al

He Served Illinois
1932-39—is Str
Heart Attack

HAD BEEN REPRES

Held Position in
State Bodies—
Spanish-Amer

Special to The New
SPRINGFIELD, I
Former United State
liam H. Dieterich of
Ill., died suddenly
room in the Abr
Hotel. He was 4.
Mr. Dieterich ret
hotel at about 9 P.
later he called his
distance. A few
while talking to the
his voice failed. E
hotel went to his ro
him dead on the
Heart disease su
cause of de

Right: The October 13, 1940 newspaper account reporting the death of Tom Mix in an automobile crash the day before.

Below:
The 1937 Cord 812 Phaeton still hooked to the tow truck that brought it to Florence.

Hollywood's elite: William Fox, Gary Cooper, Gene Autry, Carl Laemmle, Jack Warner, C.B. DeMille, Louis B. Mayer, Samuel Goldwyn, Hal Roach, Buster Keaton, Charlie Chaplin, Mickey Rooney, Clark Gable, George O'Brien, Wallace Berry, Hoot Gibson, Buck Jones, William S. Hart, Harry Carey and Sheriff Ed Echols, among many others. He was interred at Forest Lawn Cemetery in Glendale, not far from his former Fox production company and Western town site—Mixville. On October 12, 1942, two years to the day his master died, his faithful Tony, The Wonder Horse, was put to sleep as he no longer could digest food properly. He supposedly was 39.

The legacy of Tom Mix continues to this day. His Ralston radio premiums are popular on eBay; his vintage movie and circus posters bring top dollar at auctions; and his personal items, what few there are left, are priceless. The Tom Mix Museum in Dewey, Oklahoma has the largest collection of his personal items on display.

At the wash on the old Highway 89, 18 miles South of Florence, where Tom Mix died, there is a silhouette of a riderless horse and a plaque to commemorate his passing. The plaque reads:

Jan. 6, 1880—Oct. 12, 1940
In memory of Tom Mix
whose spirit left his body on this spot
and whose characterizations and portrayals
in life served to better fix memories of
the Old West in the minds of living men.

It was dedicated on December 5, 1947 by his old friend Ed Echols and Gene Autry, who grew up watching Tom Mix films.

Adela Rogers St. Johns, screenwriter, Hollywood columnist and early television personality, recalled a wonderful story of Old Hollywood. After writing two screenplays for Tom Mix Westerns (*The Broncho Twister* and *The Arizona Wildcat*) she became friends with the cowboy film star. Ms. St. Johns recalls Tom, Bill Hart and her driving to East L.A. on Sundays to visit the aging lawman Wyatt Earp. She would listen as the three historical figures sipped whiskey and talked about their two favorite subjects—William Shakespeare and Jesus. As William S. Hart once said in a farewell speech in the prologue to the rerelease of his epic western *Tumbleweeds* (1938): "Oh, the thrill of it all!"

Now he rides on heaven's range
Beyond the mountains purple haze
Down stardust trails thru golden clouds
And in that land of endless days
For it's the place where dreams come true
And the memories never die
Out there West of Yesterday
Where Tom Mix will always ride
Out there West of Yesterday
Where Tom Mix and Tony will always ride

—Don Edwards

References:

Robert S. Birchard, *King Cowboy: Tom Mix And The Movies*, Riverwood Press, Burbank, California, 1993

Gary E. Brown, "Tom Mix, King of the Cowboys Remembered," *Hollywood Studio Magazine*, Jan.-Feb. 1984, Vol. 17, No.1/2.00

Gary E. Brown, "It Happened Here: Pinal County, Arizona," *American Cowboy*, April/May 2012

Don Edwards, "West of Yesterday," *West of Yesterday* CD, Warner Brothers, Inc., Night Horse Songs, BMI, 1995

Paul E. Mix, *Tom Mix, A Heavily Illustrated Biography of the Western Star*, McFarland & Company, Inc., London, 1995

M. G. "Bud" Norris, *The Tom Mix Book*, The World of Yesterday, Waynesville, North Carolina, 1989

Buck
JONES
IN LONE PINE

by Michael Bifulco

In a career spanning three decades, Buck Jones appeared in over 150 films, many of them Westerns, before his tragic death in a fire at the Coconut Grove nightclub in Boston, Massachusetts, on November 28, 1942. Various sources report Charles Frederick Gebhardt was born in Indiana late in the 19th Century and grew up on a ranch in Indian Territory that would eventually become part of the State of Oklahoma.

With experience riding horses and a proficiency with firearms, he was a natural candidate for Army service as a teenager where he was assigned to active duty in the Philippines. Following an honorable discharge from the Army in 1909, he cultivated an interest in racing cars and flying airplanes. Hoping to become a pilot, he re-enlisted in the Aeronautical Division, U.S. Signal Corps, but soon discovered to his regret that he had to first become an officer before he would be accepted for flight training. After a second honorable discharge in 1913, he found work as a cowboy with the famous Miller Brothers 101 Ranch Show in Oklahoma. He trained horses for the Allies during WWI, joined up with the Ringling

Brothers circus, and then settled in Hollywood with his wife Odelle where he found much less dangerous work in the film industry.

Buck appeared intermittently in pictures from 1914 on, and under the name Buck Gebhardt became a member of Tom Mix's cowboy troupe around 1918. William Fox signed him to a contract as Charles "Buck" Jones with intentions to promote him as a new Western star to emulate Tom Mix. His first starring role was in *The Last Straw* (Fox, 1920).

Before the technical wizards of Hollywood learned how to make motion pictures talk, Buck Jones made three locations jaunts to Lone Pine, where he would appear in *Durand of the Bad Lands* (Fox, 1925), *The*

Above: Buck Jones and Patsy De Forest in an intense rescue scene from *Sunset Sprague* (Fox, 1920).

Opposite page: Charles "Buck" Jones strikes a pose to promote his first starring role in *The Last Straw* (Fox, 1920). The production started shooting on November 26, 1919 with Charles Swickard slated to direct (note the code "sw-2" in the lower right corner). Ironically, Charles Prichard directed the film until Denison Clift finished it and received the screen credit.

Right: Lobby one-sheet for *Durand of the Bad Lands* (Fox, 1925), the first feature Buck Jones filmed in Lone Pine.

WILLIAM FOX *presents*

BUCK JONES
IN
"DURAND OF THE BAD LANDS"

The Daring Exploits of a Beloved Outlaw

FROM THE NOVEL BY MAIBELLE HEIKES JUSTICE
DIRECTED BY LYNN REYNOLDS

Tension mounts in this thrilling scene from *Durand of the Bad Lands* starring Buck Jones.

Below: Cast and crew of *Durand of the Bad Lands*, assembled in the Alabama Hills for a studio production still.

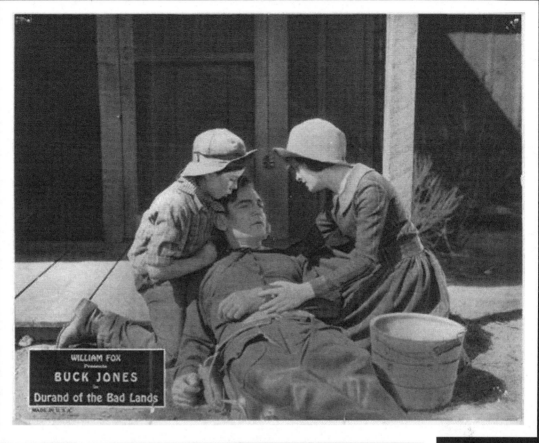

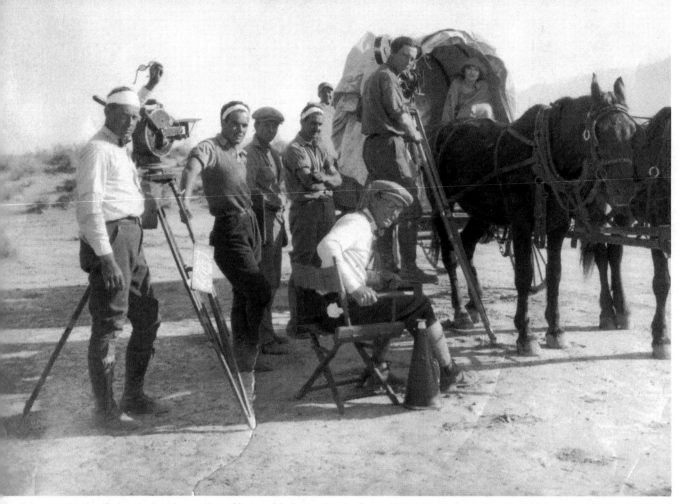

Unidentified production crew members of *Durand of the Bad Lands* posing for a publicity still with director Lynn Reynolds (seated) and leading lady Marian Nixon in the covered wagon.

Flying Horseman (Fox, 1926), and *Black Jack* (Fox, 1927). Promoted as "the daring exploits of a beloved outlaw," Buck Jones starred with Marian Nixon in *Durand of the Bad Lands*, a remake of a 1917 Dustin Farnum film that had co-starred Tom Mix. The film was one of several Jones made in which Carole Lombard would also appear. As an aside, contemporary Hollywood has been getting a lot of heat lately from critics who wonder if the flood of remakes indicates a lack of creativity. Film historians are the least surprised as the practice of recycling a story over and over again goes all the way back to the silent era. You just can't keep a good yarn down. What remains to be seen is whether or not a good yarn can be beaten to death.

Durand of the Bad Lands is the story of rancher Dick Durand (Jones) who decides to sell everything he owns to the Sheriff (Malcolm Waite) and move to Mexico. Shifty Pete Garson (Fred De Silva), disguised in Durand's left-behind clothing, goes on a crime spree that falsely implicates Durand.

Learning his reputation is being sullied, Durand returns from Mexico to clear his name. He soon meets struggling rancher Joe Gore (James Corrigan) and falls in love with his daughter, Molly (Marian Nixon). She initially rejects his affection, but eventually warms up to him after he reveals the three orphan children he saved from a deadly raid on a gold shipment for the town banker John Boyd (George Lessey). Durand executes a daring rescue of Ellen Boyd (Carole Lombard), the banker's daughter, from the clutches of Pete Garson at a nearby gold mine. Justice triumphs, Durand clears his name, enjoys the gratitude of Boyd, and finally rekindles a relationship with Molly.

Durand of the Bad Lands was written and directed

by Lynn Reynolds, based on a novel by Maibelle Heikes Justice, and released in November, 1925.

Buck Jones returned to Lone Pine within a year to appear with leading lady Gladys McConnell in *The Flying Horseman*. The film, based on the short story "Dark Rosaleen" by Max Brand, begins when Mark Winton (Jones), a cowboy and expert rider on his way to compete in a cross-country horse race, happens upon a group of local boys being threatened by abusive Bert Ridley (Walter Percival). When Mark intervenes, the bare-knuckled fight leaves Bert swearing revenge. Biding his time before the big race, Mark gets the lay of the land when he meets ranch owner Colonel Savary (Bruce Covington), the Colonel's daughter, June (Gladys McConnell), whom Bert Ridley is intent on marrying, and Happy Joe (Harvey Clark), who lives on the Colonel's ranch and is father to the boys Mark befriended.

Mark soon learns that June is planning to enter the race to win money to pay off the mortgage on the ranch, but when he discovers she is being harassed by Bert, Mark gets framed and arrested for a murder. With the help of his horse Silver Buck, Mark escapes jail, enters and wins the race, saves the Colonel's ranch, and triumphs over Bert and his gang.

Advertised as "a sixty mile an hour thrill a minute, laugh a second Western drama that will keep you on the edge of your seat" entertainment, *The Flying Horseman* was directed by Orville Dull, written by Gertrude Orr, and released in September, 1926.

Hot on the heels of *The Flying Horseman*, Buck Jones was back to work with Orville O. Dull on *Black Jack* (1927), his third and last silent film shot in Lone Pine. The script, written by Harold Shumate and based on the freshly published short story "The Broken Dollar" by Johnston McCulley in *Far West Illustrated Magazine* (January 1927), begins when Phil Dolan (Jones) befriends Nancy Blake (Barbara Bennett), a lady in distress. To repay the

WILLIAM FOX
Presents
BUCK JONES
in
THE FLYING HORSEMAN

Above: Mark Winton (Buck Jones) tames "Happy Joe's" wild mountain kids by introducing them to Boy Scouting in *The Flying Horseman* (Fox, 1926), an exciting picture made by a director with a most unfortunate name, Orville O. Dull.

Opposite page, top: After towing their broken down car back home, Mark Winton (Buck Jones) befriends an impoverished family, headed by "Happy Joe" (Harvey Clark), living in a shack in the Sierras in *The Flying Horseman* (Fox, 1926), based on the story "Dark Rosaleen" by Max Brand.

Opposite page, bottom: Lobby card featuring Buck Jones and Gladys McConnell.

Nancy Blake (Barbara Bennett), Phil Dolan (Buck Jones), and Sam Vonner (Theodore Lorch) take to the Alabama Hills in search of a lost gold mine, the map to which is stamped into a silver dollar that has been cut into three pieces, for *Black Jack* (Fox, 1927). Johnston McCulley, creator of Zorro, wrote "The Broken Dollar," the story on which this film was based, but the basic story was hardly original. J. Allen Dunn's 1920 novel, *Dead Man's Gold*, in which a map is thrice split, served as the basis for the Tom Mix film *No Man's Gold* (Fox, 1926) and (without credit) for Mix's *Rider of Death Valley* (Universal, 1932).

Phil Dolan (Buck Jones) and Sam Vonner (Theodore Lorch) duke it out as Buck's horse, Silver, watches from the distance in the climactic moments of *Black Jack* (Fox, 1927), the last of three silent films Buck Jones made in Lone Pine.

man known as "Black Jack" due to his uncanny talent with cards, Nancy uses her influence with the local Judge (George Berrell) to clear Dolan of vagrancy charges.

Crucial to the plot is a map leading to a rich mine that has been carved into three separate pieces of a single silver dollar. Nancy holds a piece of the map, but she is captured by a gang of rustlers. Dolan, also holding a piece of the map, rescues Nancy, and together they elude the rustlers on their way to the hidden mine. When the gang catches up with them and all seems lost, the Sheriff's posse arrives near the end of the final reel to save the day.

Promoted as "a whirlwind romance of the lawless days in old Nevada," *Black Jack* was released near the bitter end of the silent era in late September, 1927.

Publicity photograph of Buck Jones circa 1928.

Buck Jones, unlike many other popular stars of silent films, survived the swift transition to sound. He demonstrated a wide range of acting talent in many non-Westerns, but he did return to Lone Pine for at least three more Westerns, *Desert Vengeance* (Columbia, 1931) directed by Louis King and starring with former silent film star Barbara Bedford, *The Roaring West* (Universal, 1935) directed by Ray Taylor with Muriel Evans as his leading lady, and *Sandflow* (Universal, 1937), directed by Lesley Selander, with Lita Chevret. Buck Jones will always be affectionately remembered as a "big-hat" Western star who enriched the collective film history of our favorite movie location—Lone Pine.   □□□

Studio portrait circa 1930.

Buck Jones receives the payoff from Slim Whitaker in a scene from *Desert Vengeance* (Columbia, 1931).

Jack Hoxie in Lone Pine

by Chris Langley

The name Jack Hoxie is not exactly a household word, even in the homes of intrepid silent Western film fans like the people who usually read this publication. They have heard of him, but perhaps don't realize how often he worked in Lone Pine for Universal. Tom Mix or Hoot Gibson would probably sound more familiar than Hoxie, yet Jack Hoxie worked in the area on at least fourteen pictures. In fact, he was in town so much he participated in the life of the town.

While the legend has Hoxie born in Indian Territory (now Oklahoma), consensus is forming around a birth date of January 11, 1888 in Kansas. Jack's father was killed while attempting to break a horse, decapitated the legend says. His mother Matilda was Nez Perce and she took her family back to Idaho where, during a terrible winter, they lost much of their stock. Matilda next married Scott Stone, a stern and unbending German immigrant, and had five children before she left him. Jack hated Stone and moved to town when his stepdad sold the ranch and married a young girl, Pearl Gage. She was the first of five wives for Jack, and the marriage did not last long.

Jack soon signed on with the Dick Stanley Wild West Show. While working in the show, he met and married Hazel Panky, one of the female trick riders, and they soon had a daughter. The couple became stars of the show. As was not uncommon at that time, wild west shows often wintered in Southern California, where the cowboys sought work in movies. L.A. was not a metropolis yet, and movie making was in its infancy so Jack got in on the ground floor. Jack was one of those many artists who, when choosing between the facts and the legend, chose the legend. He did state in an interview in 1965 that after Dick Stanley was killed by a bucking bronco "I took the show to Los Angeles for Mrs. Stanley. Dick had a contract with Young Deer (James), the director, to work all the people and all the horses through the winter and then we would go back on the show tour during the summer."

Beginning as early as 1910, Jack appeared in a number of independent two-reel Western shorts released by the Pathé Exchange, but no complete record exists of how many. By 1913, Jack had quit the Wild West show and settled in California after signing an exclusive contract with The Kalem

Jack Hoxie as the title character in the ten chapter serial *Thunderbolt Jack* (1919, Arrow Film Corp.), with Marin Sais, right, whom he married shortly before production began.

Company. Over the next two years Jack appeared in at least 15 two-reel shorts and one serial, *The Hazards of Helen*, featuring Helen Holmes who was Kalem's primary star. In 1915 he had a strong supporting role in *Captain Courtesy*, a Dustin Furnum Western, his first feature. For the next few years he bounced back and forth between features and shorts, eventually reaching leading man status in 1918 in *The Wolf and His Mate*, a Universal film starring Louise Lovely.

As Hoxie biographer Edgar M. Wyatt in *The Hoxie Brothers* puts it, "From the time the elder Hoxie made his debut in pictures until he became a star, he alternated between rodeos, wild west shows, and the movies. By 1919 he was associated with Ben Wilson who was both a noted cowboy star and a director ... Eventually Ben Wilson founded an independent company called Unity Pictures. Then Hoxie went on to Sunset Pictures and made a series of five-reelers that would be distributed by Aywon Film Corporation. By 1923 his contract with Sunset was over and Jack had already signed on with Universal and he was on his way to becoming a first rate Western actor."

Sometime in the mid-teens he divorced Hazel Panky. In 1920 he married Marin Sais with whom he had worked as early as 1913 in one of her starring shorts for Kalem. Buck Rainey in his encyclopedic book *The Strong Silent Type* writes, "The marriage with Marin Sais was a good one in many respects and Marin gave Jack the polish he might have had, a thin veneer at best."

His career continued to progress and in 1921 he starred in the Ben Wilson production *Cyclone Bliss*, most likely in the Victorville area. The Museum of Western Film History in Lone Pine has a three-sheet on display for this film at this time. In 1923

Jack Hoxie (billed as Hart Hoxie) in this scene from *The Wolf and His Mate* (1918, Universal), one of the earliest features in which he had a leading role. Louise Lovely was the star of this lost film.

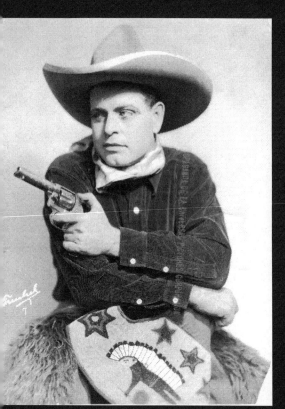

Above: One of the earliest Universal publicity photos of Jack Hoxie, circa 1920.

Below: One of several photos of Hoxie that appeared in a series of "Rough Rider" arcade cards published from the 1920s, still in print into the late 1940s.

Rough Rider Breaking in his Horse

Jack signed with Universal. This led to a series of pictures, many of which used local locations around Death Valley and the Eastern Sierra as well as Lone Pine's Alabama Hills.

Rainey enthuses, "Tall, stalwart, handsome, a fearless rider and a matchless roper and rifleman, Jack Hoxie, as he thundered across the screen in the Universal Westerns of 1923–1927, might have ridden straight out of the past. In a thousand theaters in a thousand towns Jack Hoxie and his horse Scout and his dog Bunkie provided thrill after thrill for audiences throughout rural America, making the old West come alive again for the price of a dime or a quarter."

It is thought that the earliest Hoxie feature filmed in the area might be Sunset Production's *Riders of the Law,* released in December 1922, but we lack documentation. But there is evidence that *Men in the Raw* (1923) filmed in the area. The local newspapers carried interesting notes on several of these films. One story stated, "One of the largest crowds in the history of the Lone Pine Town Hall turned out to see Jack Hoxie's production of *The Man in the Raw* (sic). This picture was filmed in the vicinity of Lone Pine and Cottonwood Lakes ... The Lone Pine Theater will show a number of these Hoxie pictures filmed here." Other area Hoxie films include *The Back Trail* (1924); *Daring Chances* (1924); *The Red Warning* (1924) and *Fighting Fury* (1924). From a Universal newsletter we know that the Hoxie unit filmed *The Red Warning* in Death Valley and Lone Pine and then moved directly to Wyoming where they finished *Man From Wyoming* (1924) before returning to Hollywood.

Men in the Raw features a teller of wild stories named Windy, played by Jack Hoxie, whose tales were usually about his personal exploits. These were told to other cowpokes as they sat around the campfire in the evening. Finally Windy is given the opportunity to prove himself when Bill Spray (Sid Jordan) and his gang decide they will steal a gold claim belonging to the father of Windy's sweetheart, Eunice Hollis, played by Marguerite Clayton.

Sadly, few of Jack Hoxie's silent films are known to exist. Silent films were printed on nitrate and when MCA took over Universal in the late 1950s, the silent Universal Westerns were deteriorating quickly. It would have taken a lot of money to restore them,

Jack Hoxie riding "Inyo," the horse that preceded "Scout" as his movie horse, in a scene from *Cyclone Bliss* (Unity Photoplays, 1921).

and the studio executives saw little future return in revenue if they did the transfer and restoration. Therefore, they gave the order to either transfer them or destroy them. MCA was stretched financially, so the order was given to destroy all of the nitrate film. Regretfully it included most of Hoxie's lifetime of work, which was judged to be of high quality by the Western fans that saw at the time.

The Back Trail (1924) is one of the two silent Lone Pine Hoxie films that have survived. A gang of crooks uses the fact that World War I veteran Jeff Prouty (Jack Hoxie) is suffering post-traumatic stress disorder to convince him he is guilty of several crimes. This allows them to manipulate him into believing he is both guilty and worthless so that they can gain control of his foster sister's property. Hoxie's real half brother, Alton Stone (Hoxie), plays a vagabond who was with Hoxie in the war. He has

switched identities with Hoxie whose real name turns out to be Prentiss. By the end of the fifth reel, Hoxie has defeated the crooks, regained his memory thanks to the Tramp, and won his foster sister Ardis Andrew's love. Eugenia Gilbert plays Ardis. Hoxie's famous horse Scout has a significant role as well in this picture.

That is a typical plot for the Hoxie Westerns produced by Universal Pictures. These plots supply plentiful opportunity for action, several twists and ample challenges for Hoxie as an actor. Besides giving the moral high road to Hoxie as Prouty defeating Gentleman Harry King (Claude Payton) and wicked ranch foreman Jim Lawton (William Lester), it dramatizes the fact that many soldiers came home from World War I suffering what we now call PTSD. That adds an additional aspect of serious meaning to this film. It is not the greatest

The Hoxie brothers on the rock, Jack (left) and Al, in a scene from *The Back Trail* (1924, Universal).

challenge presented to cowboy actors, but for the first several reels Hoxie has a glazed over, slightly vague demeanor that is effective in communicating what is first and foremost a mental and emotional condition. Countries are still learning that not all the casualties of war have only physical wounds.

An extra benefit of this film is that it survives in a very acceptable print that allows us to see the effective use made of the Lone Pine landscapes. The director is Clifford S. Smith, a talented workhorse of early Westerns. Harry Neumann as the Director of Photography probably deserves much of the credit for the composition of the shots and the creative placement of the camera.

I am speaking of one particular sequence of a stagecoach flying up Tuttle Creek Canyon Road.

Today this road is scenic and beautiful as it winds up the narrow canyon. Two lanes now, the dirt road in the film is extremely narrow, with sharp blind curves and plunging cliffs at the edge of the road that in places is outlined by rocks. I guess this represents early guard rails, but in this film they would serve little purpose in stopping the careening stage from going over at a moment's notice. To make this experience even more exciting for the audience, the camera is actually placed on the top of the stage, giving the audience the same view as the driver would have.

Many of Jack Hoxie's films ended with the hero marrying the rancher's daughter, the teacher, the heiress, or someone else who has been affected by Hoxie's characters' good acts. Maybe it was art

Two views of Tuttle Creek Road as it appears today, freshly paved. However, when it was used in numerous films from the 1920s through the 1940s, it was a very narrow dirt road, perfect for stagecoaches and wagons to be waylaid and sent careening up or down into the canyon. Along the way there are a number of large boulders and rocks tall enough and close enough to the road for the bad guys to jump onto the stagecoach as it passes.

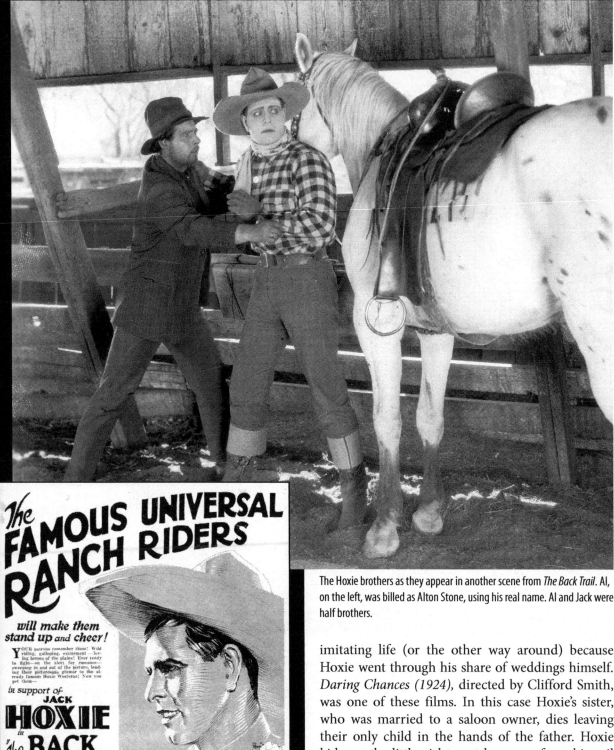

The Hoxie brothers as they appear in another scene from *The Back Trail*. Al, on the left, was billed as Alton Stone, using his real name. Al and Jack were half brothers.

The FAMOUS UNIVERSAL RANCH RIDERS

will make them stand up and cheer!

YOUR patrons remember them! Wild riding, galloping, excitement — loving heroes of the plains! Ever ready to fight — on the alert for romance — sweeping in and out of the picture, lending their picturesque glamor to the already famous Hoxie Westerns! Now you get them —

in support of

JACK HOXIE

in

'*The* **BACK TRAIL**'

Directed by
CLIFFORD S. SMITH

A UNIVERSAL PICTURE

imitating life (or the other way around) because Hoxie went through his share of weddings himself. *Daring Chances (1924)*, directed by Clifford Smith, was one of these films. In this case Hoxie's sister, who was married to a saloon owner, dies leaving their only child in the hands of the father. Hoxie kidnaps the little girl to get her away from his evil influence. He is wounded in the process and the school teacher tends to him. A rival for the teacher's hand schemes to have Hoxie lose a rodeo race. Our hero foils the dastardly plans, rescues the little girl from her second kidnapper, the rival, wins the race and the hand of the school teacher, whom he marries in the final reel. Local legend Genevieve Nafftzinger

Above: The Hoxie families prepare for a family outing. Jack and his wife Marin Sais are in the front, while Al's wife and daughter are in the back. Al is sitting on the running board.

Right:
Jack saves a little girl (Doreen Turner) from her brutal father in *Daring Chances* (1924, Universal).

had a role in this film and traveled to Hollywood to complete it.

Film researcher Karl Thiede has done a lot of work using primary sources to identify *The Red Warning* as a Lone Pine film. Directed by Robert N. Bradbury, the film has a complex plot. Hoxie portrays Philip Haver, a lone drifter who helps a young woman whose father, busy looking for a lost mine, is murdered in the desert. Fred Kohler, the chief villain, has eyes for the rancher's daughter. He kills the father so that the mortgage won't get paid, forcing the girl to marry Kohler. Hoxie organizes a gang of vigilantes to defeat the cattle rustlers. Then he finds the mine the dead rancher had been looking for.

Thiede came up with multiple mentions of the film whose working titles were "The Moon Riders" and "Riders to the Moon." He quotes *Exhibitor's*

Jack Hoxie in the Alabama Hills in one of his early films in Lone Pine *The Red Warning* (1923, Universal).

Trade Review (9/1/23, p.587) "The Moon Riders" is a working title for *The Red Warning* (released 12/17/23) "Jack Hoxie is also away on location at the present time at Lone Pine, California, for location work on 'The Moon Riders', directed by Robert North Bradbury. Those who have important parts include William Welsh, Elinor Fields, Fred Kohler and Ralph McCullough."

Thiede quoting from *Camera* (9/1/23, p19) writes, "'Riders of the Moon', a dramatic Western story written and scenarizied by Isadore Bernstein, in which Jack Hoxie, popular favorite in tales of the west, is star, has been completed at Universal City. The picture, now in the first stage of editing, was directed by Robert North Bradbury. Elinor Field is the leading lady. Others in the cast were Ralph McCullough, Ben Corbett, William Welsh, Fred Kohler, and Jim Welsh. A few miles from Lone Pine, California, on the edge of Death Valley, a location trip was made and three weeks spent in getting what is said to be the best scenic background ever seen."

"The Jack Hoxie production unit returned to Universal City after a three weeks stay in the mountains around Lone Pine and the Mojave desert filming "Riders of the Moon."

—*Exhibitor's Trade Review* 9/22/23 p770

It appears that two features were being made consecutively. The second was to be called "The Man From Wyoming." Thiede quotes from *Camera* (9/22/23, p20): "On the edge of Death Valley, where *The Red Warning*, his last starring picture was filmed, Jack Hoxie, accompanied by his "gang" of hard riding cowboys, is enjoying the climate for which the neighborhood around Lone Pine, California, is not famous. The Universal unit is filming "Wyoming", William McLeod Raine's novel, with Robert North Bradbury directing. Lillian Rich, leading woman in *Man to Man*, *The Kentucky Derby* and other big Universal pictures, is playing the leading role opposite Jack Hoxie. While on location for *The Red Warning* the Hoxie troupe encountered such pleasant little features of the country as rattlesnakes and thermometers with a habit of sticking around the "115" mark. The first bulletin received at Universal City on the present location indicated that Nature was a little kinder in the matter of temperature on this trip. The reason for the second trip to the same location is that Hoxie and his director have discovered great possibilities in the country. From a pictorial standpoint *The Red Warning* has eclipsed any other Hoxie picture."

—*Camera* 9/22/23 p20

"William Welsh, character veteran of Universal City, finished an excellent portrayal of a father role in Jack Hoxie's starring picture *The Red Warning*, and three weeks later was cast in support of Hoxie again in the picture now in production, "Wyoming". The former portrayal was highly pleasing and the new one offers him better possibilities. Robert North Bradbury had the Hoxie unit, with the star, Welsh, pretty Lillian Rich, Claude Payton, Lon Poff, George Kuwa and Ben Corbett in the regions around Lone Pine, California, near the edge of Death Valley, utilizing the inexhaustible novelties of the scenery there in adding pictorial quality to the film version of William

McLeod Raine's novel. *The Red Warning* was filmed there and the scenic features of the production drew the praise of everyone at Universal City. Jack Lawton, manager of the location department at Universal City, and William Nobles, cameraman, are coming in for a good deal of credit from Universal executives for pictorial beauty in *The Red Warning*."

—*Camera* 9/23/23 p20-21

When *The Red Warning* played at the local movie theater *The Inyo Independent* took note. The reporter posited, "Of course you all know this is the picture made in Lone Pine with Lone Pine folks doing the acting. You will be anxious to see the mugs of all the hometown guards in this picture that a twenty-mule team would not be strong enough to pull you away from the Lone Pine Hall until you've seen every inch of every reel. Come early and get a good seat."

Fighting Fury (1924) was also shot about the same time, and apparently locally. The director was not Bradbury, but old Hoxie friend Clifford Smith.

Fighting Fury (1924, Universal).

Hoxie portrays a Mexican national determined to get revenge on the three rustlers responsible for the murder of his parents. He tracks down each killer and administers his own justice. As it turns out, he has gotten a job on the ranch of one of the trio. He discovers the rancher is involved in a cattle-rustling scheme with others. With the help of a companion he is also able to end the illegal activities of these cow thieves. The famed real Oklahoman outlaw Al Jennings has a small part in this film.

The Inyo Independent, on May 17, 1926 stated, "Clever fists, a quick familiarity to ride served a young man, Jack Hoxie, well in the dangers he was to encounter and the result that he strove for was obtained in a dramatic manner in his latest Universal Western *A Roaring Adventure,* coming to the Legion Hall next Monday night July 17." The writer then reassured the local audience, "Some beautiful natural background was obtained in the Sierra Nevada Mountains where the exteriors were filmed."

Hoxie with Mary McAllister, *A Roaring Adventure* (1925, Universal).

The Inyo Independent wrote of Hoxie's film *Fighting Fury* on May 29, 1926 that it was "a peculiar melodrama of mystery and adventure in the country along the border between America and Mexico with Hoxie playing the role of a young Spanish Don whose main purpose in life is to bring an end to the careers of three crooks who murdered his parents twenty-five-year before." Of the locations used, the writer continued, "Scenery used in filming the picture is that around Lone Pine. For added photographic effects, the greater part of the picture, the action of which took place at nighttime, was filmed with a special filter screen, which has a marvelous power of imitating the exact light of the moon."

Jack Hoxie was known by many people here in Lone Pine and he left a set of spurs with Russ Spainhower's family as a thank-you gift. Russ was nicknamed "Mr. Movies" because he liaised with most of the companies on location here. The spurs remain today cherished artifacts to the family that played such an on-going part in our local film industry. Hoxie also has pictures in the family album. Joy Anderson, Russ Spainhower's daughter, as a young girl met Hoxie several times. When I was speaking with her about Jack and his then wife Marin Sais, her memories were vivid even though she had forgotten the title of the film. "I remember Jack Hoxie first. We saw more of him because of the eating facilities. A lot of the props and the extra horses were put up there at the 'Old Place' (where the Spainhower, Boyer and other families lived behind the Museum down a road now named after Hopalong Cassidy). The corrals provided room for the extra horses. "He called me 'Sweetheart.' I was pretty quiet. Sis was called

Jack Hoxie as White Elk (on the horse), an Indian chief, who falls in love with a white woman in *The Red Rider* (1925, Universal).

'Miss Quack,' because she was always talking in the background. When we would see them come in, Jack Hoxie would ask 'How's my little sweetheart?'"

Because some of Hoxie's story is lost in the shadows of the past, we can only speculate. At this time, we only know of two of the films Jack Hoxie made in Lone Pine as existent. These two silent Western films have presented unique challenges and rewards for those of us who toil to locate and identify films made in the Easter Sierra region lost to the past. The two films are *The Red Rider* (1925) and *The White Outlaw* (1925). The search for the latter actually resulted in discovering a copy of the film presumed lost and where else but on eBay.

The plot of *The Red Rider* is improbable as only silent oaters can sustain. Jack Hoxie plays White Elk, an Indian chief, a white child who was raised by his adopted tribe. White Elk is engaged to Natauka, an Indian princess played by Natalie Warfield.

In the picture he falls in love instead with a white woman. This takes care of the shadow of miscegenation of a white man marrying an Indian woman. Elk is tricked into signing away the Indian lands by unscrupulous con men. Then he is sentenced to death by his tribe. He escapes miraculously and saves the young white woman, but only because Natauka takes her place and goes to her death. The lesson of love and sacrifice is clear. Rather than an

A number of scenes from *The Red Rider* were filmed at Diaz Lake, where an Indian village was built. Here, Black Panther (Jack Pratt), a rival of White Elk, holds the white woman hostage (Mary McAllister).

Jack Hoxie, standing on the rock, in a scene in the Alabama Hills from *The Red Rider*. The Indians, with the obvious exception of the main players, were all recruited from the nearby reservation.

accurate portrait of Indian tribal culture, the film suffers a strongly romanticized white view of the "noble savage."

A very commonly seen arcade card of Hoxie in a very bad Indian wig from *The Red Rider* always looked to me like it has Diaz Lake in the background. However, it was not enough to confirm that location thus guaranteeing the film actually was made here. Then I discovered that the Eastern California Museum had at least six candids of an Indian Village easily identified as at Diaz Lake. However, the photograph's subject and action were not identified. It looked like a movie shoot, but all the photographs were long shots, epic in scope but none of the actors on horses could be identified.

A collection of seventeen stills individually identified as from *The Red Rider* came up for sale on eBay and some of them were nearly identical to the ones Eastern California Museum in Independence was holding in their collection. Not only that but many of the photographs were in the Alabama Hills and provided provenance that *The Red Rider* was definitely a Lone Pine movie that used both Diaz Lake and the Alabama Hills as locations. While the hope of getting a copy of the film is slim, the production stills allow us to create a photo documentation of nearly all the action in the film as described by the plot synopsis.

The *Mt. Whitney Observer* on August 7, 1926 carried a story about *The Red Rider*, which was going to play at the Legion Hall in Independence that week. "The picture is unique in that it is the first time that an attempt has ever been made to place on the screen the Indian's side of the story of the conflict between the red and white races in America. It tells of the inroads of the white race, of the operations of unscrupulous 'palefaces' in robbing the Indian of his lands." Often when films made locally are exhibited, the marketing blurb confirms the use of local locations. In this case it did not and thus the need for the stills mentioned above.

The White Outlaw was released in the same year and directed by the same man, Clifford Smith. The white outlaw of the title is Scout, Hoxie's horse. The wild animal does a lot of damage and Hoxie is falsely accused. He ultimately clears his name and goes out, captures and tames this wild white beast. Actor Marceline Day plays the love interest in this one.

The story of finding and identifying *The White Outlaw* was simpler and had a bit of luck involved.

Films of that time were produced for distribution on nitrate 35mm film. When the run was over, the films were not valued as future assets, and were often allowed to decay, sitting somewhere under poor storage conditions. Over time nitrate film turns into a gel related to nitroglycerin so, should there be a fire in the storage area, a very dangerous condition leading to an explosively intense fire exists. Many of these films disappeared.

Luckily a market for home distribution of these films developed and some of the ones that had made it through the ravages of time were sold for home entertainment. Produced on 16mm safety film, they were not as ill-fated. One of these 16mm prints of *The White Outlaw* turned up on eBay and although the Museum didn't win the auction, a deal was struck with the winner so that he would give

The White Outlaw

The White Outlaw (1925, Universal).

A sequence of three shots from *The White Outlaw* (1925, Universal), top, left and top of the opposite page, where Hoxie rescues the heroine, Marceline Day, from a horse stampede in the Alabama Hills.

the Museum a copy. There was no soundtrack, but in the case of *The White Outlaw* the visual quality of the print was quite good, so an important film of our country's Western film history from the early days was rescued.

When Carl Laemmle signed Jack Hoxie to star in his Western films, it turned out a great deal for both. Now most are lost but Buck Rainey writes, "The Hoxie programmers were good, according to those who can remember seeing them. His opuses were always full of fast riding and hard shooting, with a number of rough-and-tumble fights, all of which provided plenty of diversion for devotees who went for these types of screen antics."

By now his horse Scout was almost as big a star, and he had added his dog Bunkie. "Scout was more than just a horse. He had a whole repertoire of tricks which he performed in movies." Because it was Universal, Hoxie also had the advantage of the studio's high technical acumen and also some of the best action directors working at the time. These

Hoxie, Scout (the white outlaw of the title) and Marceline Day.

Scout, Scout's double and Hoxie from *The White Outlaw*.

Bunky holds the reins to Hoxie's horse in *The White Outlaw*.

included George Marshall, Robert North Bradbury, Albert Rogell, and Cliff Smith.

A review of some of the Hoxie/Lone Pine/ Universal pictures starting in 1925 is instructive. *A Roaring Adventure* (1925) was directed by Smith, and included a cast of Mary McAllister and wife Marin Sais. Francis Ford, the famous Western director John Ford's elder brother, also appears. The story is one that was repeated in other silents of the day. The son of a rancher (Hoxie) comes back from college in the East to find cattle rustlers have been plundering the ranch. Hoxie passes himself off as a plain old cowpuncher. In the last reel Hoxie exposes the thieves with the help of the local sheriff. The college educated next generation coming home signals the changing West with accompanying anxiety.

Clifford Smith directed the next Hoxie/Lone Pine/Universal Western *The Demon*, (1926) as well.

A gang of marauders, led by Bat Jackson, is draining a ranch of its value. A silent partner in the ranch, Hoxie assumes the disguise of an ex-con to infiltrate the gang. When the rustlers plundering all the ranches in the valley learn of Hoxie's true identity, they try to kill him. With the help of a posse things are set right.

Once more it is Smith directing Hoxie, with Olive Hasbrouck, as co-owners of a ranch through strange happenstance of inheritance. This film has a foreshadowing title of *Six Shootin' Romance* (1926). The "saucy socialite" Donaldeen (Hasbrouk) becomes angry with Hoxie, but when she rejects a married lustful neighbor, the cad kidnaps her. Hoxie rides to her rescue and discovers that they actually love each other after all.

The next outing for Hoxie in Lone Pine was directed by Al Rogell. It is the 1926 vehicle *Wild*

Hoxie, with an unidentified player, returns to the Alabama Hills for *The Demon* (1926, Universal).

Horse Stampede (1926). The co-star was Fay Wray in her pre-*King Kong* days. Marin Sais was also credited. This was the last film they were to make together. They divorced soon after the production ended. The plot has Hoxie rounding up one thousand horses with the help of Scout so that he can marry the woman he loves. There is a rival named Champion. Through plot contrivances, the competitor is killed in a stampede but a mysterious woman arrives claiming to be his wife. And so his despicable nature is revealed even after death. Hoxie is able to marry his true sweetheart played by Wray.

Opposite page: *The Wild Horse Stampede* (1926, Universal).

Olive Hasbrouck and Jack Hoxie, *A Six Shootin' Romance* (1926, Universal).

A
Blue Streak
Western

JACK HOXIE
IN
A SIX SHOOTIN'
ROMANCE

STORY BY
Ruth Comfort Mitchell

DIRECTED BY
Clifford S. Smith

4445-1

Dell Henderson directs *The Rambling Ranger* (1927) in a change-of-pace film that, according to critics and fans at the time, lacked action. Hoxie adopts a baby and there is much footage of the two interacting while a ne'er-do-well is influencing the mothers of the community to get the child taken away. The working title was "The Fighting Foundling" and the Museum of Western Film History has a wonderful still with the title and a very small shadowy yet clearly identifiable Mt. Whitney in the background. This provides irrefutable evidence the film was produced locally.

Al Rogell is back to direct the final Hoxie/Lone Pine/Universal film *Rough and Ready* (1927). Again we are focused on a land swindle, a popular plot device of the time. I am not certain if land swindles

Fay Wray, before she became a major star in the 1930s, appeared in a number of B Westerns for Universal and other film companies. Here she is with Jack Hoxie, with Bunky, in *The Wild Horse Stampede*.

Jack Hoxie rescues "Royal Highness" in this scene from the *The Rambling Ranger* (1927, Universal).

were as common in the society of the old west as their film appearances would indicate. Again there is an Eastern capitalist and a ranch foreman involved, and ranch hand Hoxie uncovers it in the nick of time. The Easterner named Manning lends the ranch owner the money to pay off the mortgage using the cattle as collateral. When oil is discovered on the land, the conman convinces the ranch foreman to organize cattle rustling. Luckily, Hoxie is able to thwart the plan, and just for icing on the cake marry the rancher's daughter.

Hoxie's career luck changed in 1927. Rainey explains, "Something happened between Jack and Universal in 1927, with the result that Jack tore up his contract. It was like signing his own death warrant. From that day he was washed up in movies though he would make a few." Jack would go on to make six low budget, independent sound Westerns

originally meant to star Ken Maynard. Ironically, Maynard withdrew from these films when he signed a contract with Universal, leaving the producers at short notice without a star.

With the end of his film career, he returned to the wild west shows and the circus where his career had begun. He married his fourth wife Dixie Starr, who was a stuntwoman and trick rider featured in the wild west shows with him. Things were over for the film hero from the sense of being a large star.

After World War II, with his fifth wife Bonnie Showalter whom he had married in 1944, he bought a dude ranch in southern Arizona while he continued with the circus. In the early 1950s, the dude ranch burned and Jack retired from the circus and he and Bonnie moved to a small ranch in Mulberry, Arkansas. With the onset of leukemia he moved to Keyes, Oklahoma to a small place his mother had owned. He died on March 17, 1965 in Elkhart, Kansas

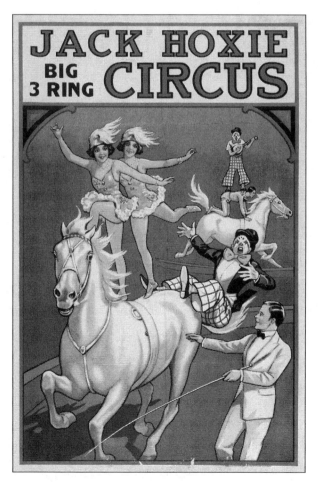

at the age of 77. It had been fully three decades since his movie career, and yet for those Western fans who still remembered and cared, he was one of the great silent film cowboys.

NOTE: *It seems likely that other films made by Jack Hoxie for Universal also shot scenes in Lone Pine, Death Valley or the Sierra Nevada. Consequently we look forward to any confirming evidence allowing us to add to the Hoxie filmography.* ☐☐☐

HOOT
GIBSON

"LUCKY
TERROR"

in *LONE PINE*

by Richard W. Bann

"No gun, huh?"
"Ha! I never carry one."

Born on a ranch near a Sioux Indian Reservation in Tekamah, Nebraska, Edmund Richard Gibson (1892-1962) grew up riding, roping, fighting and shooting. "I used to go out in caves and hunt owls," he would explain. "The kids started hollering 'Hoot' at me and the name stuck." By another account, he acquired the cognomen as a boy making deliveries on his bicycle for the Owl Drug chain. Gibson himself told both stories, depending on the situation. Today at least the name lives on; as just one of several examples, there is an NASA astronaut named Hoot Gibson.

"The Hooter" ran away with a circus at age 13 in 1905, then became a cowpuncher, wrangler, bronc-buster, and bulldogger, competing in wild west shows and touring the rodeo circuit. In 1910, as a seasonal sideline, this young drifter entered the brand new movie industry and began performing stunts, trick riding and bit roles in Western short subjects. He always claimed he was the movies' first stunt man. Perhaps his earliest screen appearance was for D. W. Griffith in a one-reeler featuring Mary Pickford and Mack Sennett.

Competing in Oregon's famous annual Pendleton Round-Up in 1912, Gibson was awarded a diamond-studded belt as "World's All-Around Champion Cowboy."

The following year he married—or did he?—his first of four alleged wives, who as Helen Gibson replaced Helen Holmes in *The Hazards of Helen,* a noted serial which ran for 119 episodes over three years. Gibson doubled the actress in many scenes. During 1914-17 he also doubled, supported, and performed stunt work in Westerns starring Tom Mix and Harry Carey—some directed by John Ford, then billed as "Jack Ford."

After service for the Army Tank Corps in France during World War I, Universal Pictures signed Gibson in 1919 to star in a series of lighthearted, two-reel Westerns. He graduated to feature films in 1921. His first two were directed by his old friend, Ford. Both being Irish, and salty, with fiery tempers, they had several interests in common. Besides drinking.

They'd worked together in movies before, many times, daring to start out as stuntmen together. This was back when they shared a room at the Virginia Apartments in Hollywood.

Over the next decade, Hoot Gibson was Universal's number one Western star, in charge of his own unit, Jewel Productions. At his peak, the studio paid him the reported sum of $14,500 per week, out of which he remitted nominal taxes. He could afford plenty of oats, among other things. Only Tom Mix's reputed top salary, which, depending on the source, ranged from $17,500 to $20,000 per week at Fox, eclipsed Gibson during the silent era. He spent money recklessly, drove a Rolls Royce, threw wild parties, and bought a huge ranch at Saugus near Newhall where he staged rodeos that were often filmed and turned up as stock footage in Westerns. One example was the Tim Holt shoot-'em-up made in Lone Pine, *Rider From Tucson* (1950); in one scene, Gibson, himself, can be glimpsed from behind.

Hoot Gibson was featured in a number of Harry Carey shorts. Here he is sitting on a horse directly behind Carey and his wife Olive Carey in a production company still from *The Wedding Guest* (1916, Bison Motion Picture Co.). Director Jacques Jaccard is kneeling on the right behind the megaphone and Edmund Cobb is on the horse second from left.

UNIVERSAL FEATURE EXTRAORDINARY~

CARL LAEMMLE OFFERS

HOOT GIBSON IN "ACTION"

By J. Allen Dunn
Directed by Jack Ford

FIVE REEL SPECIAL

Hoot Gibson's first starring feature in 1921.

Ironically, the UCLA Film and Television Archive preserves and stores classic films in a facility located there today. The inventory includes 35mm elements on seven sound-era Gibson titles, though none has been preserved to date. Foremost among them: top grade budget bronc quickies *The Local Bad Man* (1932) and *Sunset Range* (1935).

Exhibitors booked many of the Hooter's early, breezy, outdoor adventures as solid "A" features. They were branded as Universal Jewel special releases. Extra time, money and production polish were lavished on these efforts. Unfortunately, as with most Universal silents, the majority of Gibson's best films made for the studio are lost, carelessly destroyed on purpose. All the more reason to restore and preserve nitrate elements on the two surviving horse operas named above—just as Gibson, himself, pleads throughout one of them, *Sunset Range,* "And I'll tell ya the reason why!"

Bringing with him a company of approximately 75 people each time, as best can be determined, he shot at least eight of these celebrated Universal productions amidst the scenic grandeur of Lone Pine: *The Ridin' Kid From Powder River,* (1924), *The Silent Rider* (1927), *Hey! Hey! Cowboy* (1927), *Clearing The Trail* (1928), *The Danger Rider* (1928), *Points West* (1929), *Spurs* (1930), and *Trailin' Trouble* (1930)—his pal Art Acord's only talkie. Gibson himself flew his own plane back and forth to location shooting in Lone Pine, where, according to

Owens Valley newspapers, he always made friends with everyone.

Among his young fans were future B–Western stars Gene Autry and Monte Hale, who said of his hero with whom he became friends until Gibson passed, "He had personality personified, a real gentleman, a prankster. One helluva man, ol' Lefty, the cowboy with dancin' eyes." He was also the favorite saddle ace of Roy Rogers growing up.

Gibson's equestrian exploits contributed to his popularity and were always a marvel to behold. He often rode a stunt horse named Goldie, but unlike other cowboy icons, Gibson did not regularly feature a billed trick horse in his oaters. Ken Maynard had Tarzan, Roy Rogers had Trigger, while Hoot usually went to Hollywood's ace trainer of horse flesh, "Fat" Jones, to merely rent one. "I always used a cow pony," he explained late in life. "When I went plugging down a hill, I wanted to be sure I had a horse that'd get me to the bottom."

Away from movies, Gibson's attire was civilian, and expensive. Any time discussing him, Gene Autry never failed to mention how shocked he was

Hoot wearing the expensive civilian attire Gene Autry thought inappropriate for a cowboy star of his magnitude.

Morning scene with Kathleen Key for *Hey! Hey! Cowboy* (1927).

Stationary rider. Saddle pals Hoot Gibson and Otis Harlan demonstrate equestrian skills for a tyke not going far named Wendell Franklin in this scene from *The Silent Rider* (1927).

Scenic Lone Pine exteriors frame smash-bang action for a rodeo scene in the all-talking bronc opera *Spurs* (1930). Early in his career, Hoot Gibson competed in rodeos, later he promoted and staged them on his own huge ranch property.

A natty looking Hoot Gibson sails to Hawaii with wife Sally Eilers for her role in the earliest extant Charlie Chan mystery, *The Black Camel* (1931). Also on board, pictured, and in the cast, are Bela Lugosi and Warner Oland. Waving his hat, Oland is partially obscuring the director, Hamilton MacFadden (left elbow on the railing). He was a graduate of the Harvard Law School, who distinguished himself by helming not only the early Charlie Chans for Fox, but also Tom Mix in *The Fourth Horseman* (1932) for Universal, and George O'Brien in the definitive *Riders Of The Purple Sage* (1931). Courtesy of Ronald V. Borst/Hollywood Movie Posters.

to meet Mr. Gibson for the first time and discover the way he dressed away from movie cameras. "Right then," Autry would say, "I resolved that whatever I wore would have at least a western touch. The kids expected that."

In April of 1931, Gibson accompanied wife Sally Eilers on a cruise to Honolulu for her role in the wonderful Charlie Chan whodunit, *The Black Camel*, with Warner Oland, Bela Lugosi, and Robert Young. Also on board, and staying at the same Royal Hawaiian Hotel, was the vacationing family of Stan Laurel. His wife, Lois, said Gibson was the surprise

of the trip, impressing everyone with his generosity and personality. "He loved life," she said, "and the main thing I recall, he was always smiling." Every photograph on the ship, and at the hotel, showed him in pricy designer suits. For the movie cameras, however, in his own films, he dressed like a rube, "the hired hand," author Don Miller wrote. In *Lucky Terror*, Hoot wears the same shirt in every scene, and his left sleeve is torn.

As another hallmark, Gibson's pictures were novel because they were leisurely paced, often prized comedy over action, and downplayed violence.

The star worked closely with writers and directors to shape stories to his special talents, interests, and offbeat characterization. He had an ingratiating, relaxed aura. His dramatic ability was limited, but he stayed within his range where he could generate laughter effortlessly. Audiences related to his regular, everyman quality and bantering style. Hoot was plain looking, but the way his blue eyes registered on black and white film offered a well-defined appearance.

His all-thumbs persona was carefree, cheerful, resourceful, amiable, peaceable, good-humored, fumbling, easygoing, nonchalant, unglamorous, understated and unique among cowboy heroes. Because, among other things, he seldom carried a gun or engaged in fisticuffs (though he could definitely deliver on both skills when required). "No gun, huh?" asks a tough guy of the befuddled Hooter in *Lucky Terror.* "Ha! I never carry one," he smiles,

In what was the norm in most Hoot Gibson films, his character is always caught in some kind of mischief. Here he is caught trying to steal a chicken in *A Trick of Hearts* (1928, Universal). Blackface comic Heinie Conklin and George Ovey look on.

With the snow-capped Sierras barely visible in the distance, Hoot Gibson and Dorothy Gulliver in a scene from *Clearing The Trail* (1928), shot at the Lubken Ranch, south and west of the town of Lone Pine. As with most Universal silent subjects, sadly, this one, too, is a lost film.

hoping, as always, to be disarming and avoid trouble. Did contemporaries Buck Jones, George O'Brien, or John Wayne ever *avoid* trouble?

Off-screen was a different story. There Gibson was extremely competitive, and daring—with a long history of auto, aviation and motorcycle racing. He was prone to fistfights to the point of being barred from several restaurants and saloons in Hollywood. The hard-drinking Gibson and Ford fought at least once. It started when Ford smashed a piano stool over Gibson's head, "And then he came at me with a bottle," Ford recalled decades later when the two were making *The Horse Soldiers (1959).*

That other old Universal mainstay, Art Acord, had the reputation of being the toughest and most

reckless of all 1920s sagebrush performers, but according to director Breezy Eason, the rough-and-tumble Acord could never do better than a draw in the many donnybrooks he had with his friend Gibson. Tim McCoy told film historian Kevin Brownlow, "They'd just stand up and beat the hell out of each other. They loved it." Another director, Bruce "Lucky" Humberstone (who was given that nickname at one of Hoot's parties), told of the time Gibson brawled in a bar with Tom Mix—known to be a regular event for these two. Both were about 5'9," amateur boxers, and on this particular occasion, inebriated. Mix had to be carried out to an ambulance on a stretcher. Yet the genial "Hooter," early-on billed by Universal in their comic capers

Another Universal cowboy movie star had a long history with Hoot. Art Acord and Hoot went back to the rodeo days when Hoot was a teenager and the drinking bouts and brawls the two participated in are legendary. Here is a postcard Art sent, inscribed "When you are out having funn (sic) think off (sic) this old Drunking Bum—Art Acord."

as "The Smiling Whirlwind," remained friends with Acord, Ford, Mix and everyone else.

During the silent era, audiences flocked to see real-life cowpunchers like Gibson on movie screens. But times were changing. After one season of talking pictures, Universal temporarily lost faith in horse operas. In a distinct comedown, Gibson signed with M.H. Hoffman's Allied Pictures for the 1931–32 season and beyond. Though some of these pictures were entertaining models of low-keyed humor, with Gibson his usual homespun, innocent self, this decision was a mistake. When Universal wanted their star back, Hoffman declined to release him. Litigation ensued. When the dust settled, the opportunity at Universal had been lost (to Ken Maynard). So Gibson drifted down the trail to another independent for a pair of superior First Division Westerns in 1935, then on to RKO Radio for two fine all-star specials, the Three Mesquiteers film *Powdersmoke Range,* and *The Last Outlaw,* based on the John Ford story.

The trend was towards musical Westerns and Gibson was finding it rough going in a market then already saturated by cowpokes. Plus contractual restrictions and commitments on the sawdust circuit had combined to keep him intermittently off theater marquees across the land.

As did his accident. In 1933 Hoot competed with his close friend and future co-star a decade later on the Trail Blazers series, Ken Maynard, in a special match race for the Will Rogers Trophy at the National Air Races. Festivities were held before a huge crowd where stands LAX today. Aviatrix Amelia Earhart participated in events that day as well. Banking his J-5 Swallow plane high in the sky for a sharp turn, Hoot struck a guide pole with his wing tip, crashed his bi-plane, and was pinned in the cockpit. He suffered serious injuries. The plane was destroyed. The story made headlines worldwide. He cracked ribs, fractured three vertebrae, fractured his leg, sustained a concussion, and lost some teeth—sending the daredevil to the hospital for nearly six

Hoot Gibson in *Spurs* (1930), out among the great granite boulders of Lone Pine's spectacular Alabama Hills.

months, and out of the public eye. For the rest of his life, Gibson walked with a slight limp.

Facing all these distractions, by 1935, even though he'd made over 200 pictures, Gibson wound up being pretty much absent from movie screens. As a result he was relatively unknown to the newest successive generation of young moviegoers, focused on an increasingly glutted Western field. Still he was a name to be reckoned with. In the first-ever, annual ordinal ranking of top ten Western box-office attractions, as conducted that year by *The Motion Picture Herald,* Hoot Gibson placed ninth.

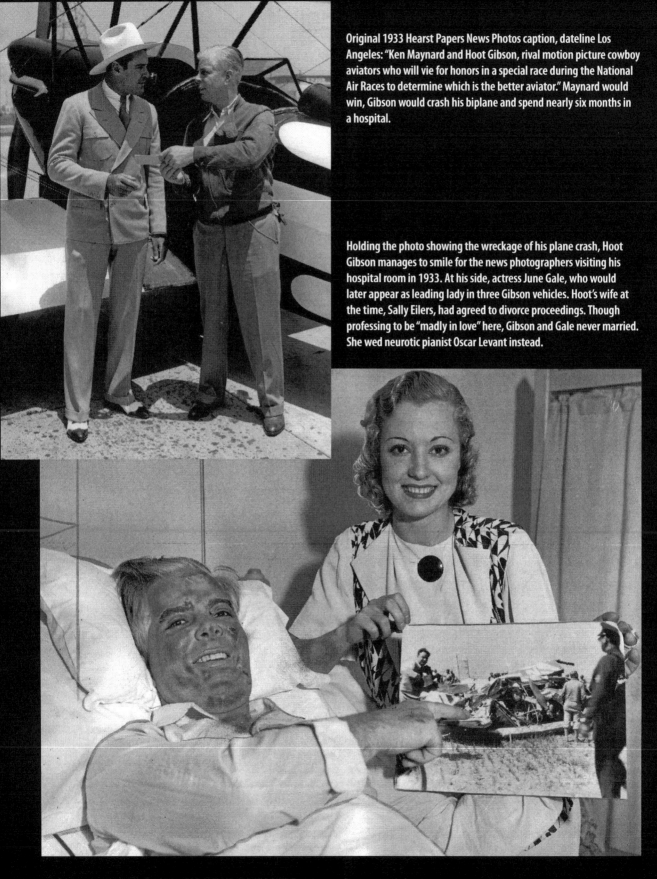

Original 1933 Hearst Papers News Photos caption, dateline Los Angeles: "Ken Maynard and Hoot Gibson, rival motion picture cowboy aviators who will vie for honors in a special race during the National Air Races to determine which is the better aviator." Maynard would win, Gibson would crash his biplane and spend nearly six months in a hospital.

Holding the photo showing the wreckage of his plane crash, Hoot Gibson manages to smile for the news photographers visiting his hospital room in 1933. At his side, actress June Gale, who would later appear as leading lady in three Gibson vehicles. Hoot's wife at the time, Sally Eilers, had agreed to divorce proceedings. Though professing to be "madly in love" here, Gibson and Gale never married. She wed neurotic pianist Oscar Levant instead.

But the downward progression continued, and the falling star would never make the list again. Had there been such a regular poll during the 1920s, only Tom Mix would have surpassed him in the popularity sweepstakes.

In mid-1935, the now aging cowpoke contracted with another minor state-rights producer, Walter Futter. He was eight years' Gibson's junior. This entrepreneur had a long history making hundreds of curiosity-type short subjects. Futter formed Diversion Pictures for the Gibson project and executed a releasing arrangement with First Division, the distribution arm of Pathé, for a series of what the trade ads termed "eight whoopee Westerns, pre-sold through exploitation campaigns and dealer tie-ups." Before Futter could complete his product delivery, however, the First Division film exchanges were absorbed by Grand National Pictures, and their revised deal called for six units instead of eight.

Since his series was leveraged on the cheerful adventures of Hoot Gibson, for the initial entry, *Frontier Justice*, Futter hired as his director Bob McGowan, veteran of the Our Gang comedies. (Leo McCarey's brother, Ray, had just helmed Gibson's first-rate *Sunset Range*.) Second effort was *Swifty*, pairing the Hooter with his off-screen inamorata of three years, June Gale and, in an exception to the rule, featuring "Starlight, the Wonder Horse," usually ridden by Jack Perrin, but also seen keeping company with John Wayne, Bob Livingston, and his brother, Jack Randall. Series interiors—and next up *Lucky Terror* would suffer from too many of them— were shot at Argosy Pictures Corporation, which rented space at the General Service Studios on Las Palmas Avenue in Hollywood.

Scenic still photo posed out in the Alabama Hills during the opening scenes of *Lucky Terror*. Hoot Gibson is about to lose both his hat and horse, in an unfair exchange with George Chesebro.

Named to direct and craft the screenplay for *Lucky Terror* was Alvin J. Neitz, who took screen credit as Alan James. This veteran helmsman of cowpoke programmers and serials had a fine record of success, particularly on 14 top grade pictures with Ken Maynard, not the easiest to manage. James was philosophical about his career, "While some people might fall from the big time and end up on Poverty Row, nobody on the row makes it to the big time, or should even try." And certainly not with *Lucky Terror* on one's resumé, though it does satisfy just fine, thank you, as an unpretentious B Western.

Principals in the cast for *Lucky Terror* were announced in the trade paper *Variety*'s December 11 issue of 1935. Wally Wales, given a small character part, was just past the days of starring roles in Poverty Row cheapies for lowly independents. He was always a welcome and distinctive addition to any company of actors. Born Floyd Alderson, he'd recently been billed as Walt Williams, and was shortly to be re-christened as Hal Taliaferro. An authentic cowpuncher from Wyoming, he drifted into movies during the teens, supporting Tom Mix. After a long and versatile career in films, he returned to work as a real-life, ranching cowboy.

Far down the list of any casting director's preferred comedy sidekicks was Frank Yaconelli. His contributions were limited to playing the accordion and speaking in an Italian dialect, which in other Western quickies was often perverted to pass for a Mexican dialect. Either way, he specialized in malaprops. Futter's budget could not afford anyone better.

If not Roy Barcroft, then the prolific, dark-haired, mustachioed Charley King was the definitive B-Western heavy. The burly King's omnipresent characters were often called "Blackie." In *Lucky Terror*, however, the redoubtable rogue was assigned a cuddly comedy role as a perpetually inebriated attorney. In a sad irony, he died of complications from cirrhosis of the liver and chronic alcoholism in 1957.

The ever-scowling George Chesebro (spelled on screen as "Cheesbro") plays an important part in the early goings of *Lucky Terror*, delivering the despicable villainy he was known for in hundreds of sagebrushers, even though, this time, he was innocent of any wrongdoing!

Short, portly, veteran character actor Robert McKenzie was born in Ireland, and wherever he worked in movies, look for his personal stock company of family members: wife Eva, daughters Ida Mae (later the producer on TV's original *Hollywood Squares* program), Ella (spouse of character actor Billy Gilbert), and Fay (married to actor Steve Cochran, then screenwriter Tom Waldman). They can all be found in *Lucky Terror*. Fay McKenzie was 17 at the time. At age 15, she was Wally Wales' leading lady in *Sundown Trail* (1934). Her Lone Pine credits include *Down Mexico Way* (1941), opposite Gene Autry. When her second husband began collaborating with director-producer Blake Edwards, she took roles in the latter's films, including *Breakfast At Tiffany's* (1961), *The Party* (1968), and *S.O.B.* (1981). She is 97 today.

The principal feminine interest was provided by Lona Andre. Her real name was Launa (pronounced

1933 Paramount publicity photo showcasing Kathleen Burke, Gail Patrick, Verna Hillie, and Lona Andre. Miss Burke is the one who bested Miss Andre to play "The Panther Woman" in *The Island Of Lost Souls*, censored in England for being "against the laws of nature."

La-una) Andersen. She was from Nashville, which accounts for the pleasing accent. In 1932, Paramount Pictures staged a national "Panther Woman" contest, which drew her interest. The studio was trying to cast a part in their film, *Island Of Lost Souls*. Hard to fathom, but she failed to win that competition. This did lead to a contract with Paramount, however, and her selection as a Wampas Baby Star the same year. She was selected along with Ruth Hall, Ginger Rogers, Gloria Stuart, who lived to be 100 and played the "old lady" in *Titanic* (1997), and Mary Carlisle, now nearing her 102nd birthday.

Like her friends Toby Wing and Grace Bradley (long time Lone Pine guest, Mrs. William Boyd) at Paramount, Miss Andre spent more time posing for seductive, killer photographs than making movies. In black and white still photos, her red hair and blue eyes were distinctive. She was beautiful, but her look and manner were often hard. She *was* hard. Married several times, she divorced actor Edward Norris after four days. Following her tenure with Paramount, she freelanced in pictures with Buster Keaton, Laurel & Hardy, and in Westerns opposite Ken Maynard and Buck Jones. Making *Lucky Terror*, she was 20, Mr.

After retrieving the saddlebags with the gold, Hoot is hiding from the gang pursuing the man who tried to steal Hoot's knee. Looking at the ground around and the snow, it makes sense that every effort would be made to keep the principal players dry.

Gibson was 43. Since Gibson was more deadpan comedian than actor, the age disparity—despite the Hooter's boyish charm and ready smile—made any semblance of romance difficult.

Lona Andre left movies after the war, and joined Lockheed Corporation in the aerospace industry. She rose through the ranks to a managerial position in a career lasting three decades. She started out inspecting work performed on planes, and was the only woman doing it. She never discussed her movie career with colleagues.

The lady still looked amazing in 1990, though she evinced no vanity concerning her appearance, proud of the fact that she'd not resorted to plastic surgery of any kind. Nor did being remembered by movie fans interest her. She could be sweet, and she could be mean, and said so. She could talk tough in movies, and also at age 75 in restaurants, slapping her hand down on the table to emphasize a point. What a pistol. She wanted it understood how aggressive she'd been about doing her own stunts whenever possible. In every movie she made, men wanted to sleep with her. "They asked plenty," she said, fire in her eyes, just as in her films. "I always made it clear what the boundaries were; you know, 'Not with *this* dame, buddy.'"

Going through stills from *Lucky Terror,* Miss Andre commented, "I never saw this one. I never saw most of (the movies I made). Hoot Gibson was fun, a pleasure to be with. He was a thorough professional, but he didn't care about much—happy-go-lucky guy. Polite. Nice guy. He was too old for me, though. One time I needed money, and I took a job in a Western. Maybe it was this picture,

Lucky Terror shot posed strictly to accommodate the still photographer and maximize exploitation value, because when the oppressors, villains and pluguglies find that saddle Jack Rockwell is holding, Hoot Gibson has no part in the scene. A good trick on us.

I have no idea now. I mentioned it to my agent in his office. He was sitting there with his feet up. He complained at me, said, 'Why do a stupid thing like working in a Western?' I got angry, told him I needed the money, and he wasn't getting me any work. The argument escalated to the point where I took out my cigarette case, and threw it at him, drawing blood on his forehead.... I received a letter of termination the next day."

The story opens high up in the empty rocks of the Alabama Hills, where Hoot Gibson is innocently drifting along, minding his own business, when he happens upon a chase and gun battle. Jack Rockwell and his gang of killers (including Wally Wales and Art Mix) are riding across the snow-covered flats in hot pursuit of George Chesebro. He ditches them, but sees his weary mount is all in. So when by chance

he runs into Gibson (who, unlike all other cowboy stars, tries to stay out of any fighting), Chesebro doubles back, gets the drop on him as he hides, and forces a swap of transportation. But Hoot's panic-stricken horse objects, bolts, and rears up. Chesebro fails to handle him, and in the terrifying struggle is accidentally thrown over a steep precipice to his death on the rocks far below. Gibson discovers gold dust in Chesebro's saddlebags, and hides it nearby until he can locate the rightful owner before proceeding on his way.

Then he crosses paths with, and comes to the aid of, a traveling patent medicine show that has become stranded. Their wagon has lost a wheel. This enterprise is operated by Charles Hill (as Doc Haliday), assisted by alleged musician Frank Yaconelli, and the show's featured attraction, lovely

Hoot Gibson to the rescue of stranded medicine show performers as enacted by Lona Andre, Charles Hill, and Frank Yaconelli. When retakes and added scenes were called for in *Lucky Terror*, they were filmed in the popular Garden of the Gods section at the Iverson Ranch overlooking Chatsworth, as shown here, rather than spend the extra time and money to return all the way to Lone Pine.

Frontier skulduggery: Jack Rockwell, Lona Andre, Frank Yaconelli, Hoot Gibson, Charles Hill, George Kesterson (Art Mix), Fargo Bussey, and Wally Wales (Hal Taliaferro) in a tense confrontation filmed for *Lucky Terror*.

Lona Andre. Turns out she is the niece of the man whose death Gibson just witnessed. She and her uncle own the Bonanza Mine together, although she has never seen it, nor does Hoot reveal that her relative is dead.

After aiding the troupe when Rockwell and his desperados happen by and try to question them, Gibson, as "Lucky Carson," signs on as a sharpshooter and joins the act as "Lucky Terror" for their next engagement in the nearby town of Poker Flats. There he is accused of killing Chesebro, whose corpse has just been discovered. Sheriff Bob McKenzie arrests Gibson. In need of legal representation during the inquest, Hoot is directed to the jail cell where Charles King, the town drunk, is sleeping one off. He is an attorney. Never before having defended an innocent client, counsel advises Gibson to flee, which the prisoner does, so that when he is acquitted by the

coroner's jury, he is unaware of the outcome. On the run, Gibson retrieves the gold dust and re-hides it in the hopper of the stamp mill at the Bonanza Mine.

When Andre first inspects the mine, she finds her uncle's diary which (1) discloses that except for the bags of gold extracted, the mine is now worthless, and (2) incriminates Rockwell. She rushes to fetch the sheriff, and together with Gibson riding hell-bent in a fine display of his saddle prowess, they vanquish Rockwell and his gang and herd them off to jail. In a comedy tag, the snake-oil salesman Hill and his assistant Yaconelli coincidentally mix up a batch of their phony elixir in the hopper where Hoot has dumped the ore, and believe they have discovered a new way to pan for gold.

Though it hardly matters, the narrative's conclusion is muddled and not clear. Of course neither is the matter of how Charles King passed the bar exam.

Or why anyone believed Charles Hill's interminable medicine show patter would help the picture. "City feller," rightly scoffs a frowning resident of Poker Flats.

Producer Futter had a peculiar notion for music scoring. Most of the series entries carried annoying romantic, semi-classical cues which had no place on the prairies of outdoor action adventure pictures and only got in the way. On January 29, 1936, *Variety* declared, "Abe Meyer cleffing musical background for Walter Futter's *Lucky Terror.*" But in fact the story would feature no incidental scoring, except during the opening and closing credits. This was a happy addition by subtraction for *Lucky Terror.*

The movie was released on a state rights basis by First Division (or Grand National, depending upon which trade paper is consulted) on February 20, 1936. Issued third in the series, it was the only one utilizing the beautiful scenery offered by Lone Pine, and represented Hoot Gibson's last excursion into the rocky terrain of the Alabama Hills.

Lucky Terror was hardly the old Hooter's best work, but he remained happy-go-lucky as always, and this escapade was easily the most interesting of the six modest Futter films. As Gibson had long bossed his own unit, he must have explained to Futter, with only a meager allotment to spend making this series, that for the cost of travelling to Lone Pine, they could gain extra polish and inordinate production values filming exteriors in the lush setting of the Alabama Hills against the spectacular framing of the snow-covered Eastern Sierras.

Shooting dates are not available, but the company figures to have visited Lone Pine during December or early January. Galloping through foothills filled with snow on the north end of Movie Road at the base of Mount Whitney, riders are shown in the opening footage wearing jackets, and their breath is visible in some scenes. It did not appear they were working at a particularly high altitude; it was just winter, and cold. Such impressive snow-covered footage is rare, not only for Lone Pine films, but throughout the entirety of B Westerns.

Retakes and additional scenes were deemed necessary for the opening and closing chase sequences. But it was too expensive to drive half-a-day each way back to Lone Pine. So the company settled for shooting the required footage at the Iverson Movie Ranch in Chatsworth, much nearer to Hollywood. For anyone who has visited either location, the cross-cutting between the differing exteriors is obvious.

The toughest reviews of the trade were almost always those penned by the hard-bitten critics for *Variety.* True to form, theirs called *Lucky Terror* "one of the dullest, most absurd outdoor mellers in many weeks. Even Hoot Gibson's presence fails to cover up roving direction, slovenly acting, sluggish pace and specious story or development of it. Major portion of acting would indicate director James had his back turned most of the time. It's that terrific. Few bright spots are when Gibson swings into action or does a wild dash on his bronc. Lona Andre poses nicely

Between scenes of RKO's hard to see and undeservedly unsung *The Last Outlaw* (1936), based on the John Ford story. According to the studio caption, "the cream of the movie industry's cowboy crop" entertain Margaret Callahan with a lot of tall tales. Harry Carey appears to be spinning this one. He and Gibson were already friends for a quarter century. Standing at right is Tom Tyler.

Behind the scenes on the set of *Powdersmoke Range* (1935, RKO), Hoot visits with Boots Mallory, the film's leading lady.

and is pretty . . . (She) does a cooch that not only is awkward, but in poor taste."

So *Variety* didn't care for it.

Had his back turned?

During the mentioned dance which Lona Andre performs as a come-on for the rubes, Yaconelli asks Hoot what he thinks of the show business. Glancing at her, he scratches his head and says, "If I said what I thought, I'd probably lose my job."

Motion Picture Daily filed a more positive notice: "An average Western, this has all the requisite action and romance which will please children and fans. It is definitely for dual bills. The performances by Gibson and Miss Andre are convincing. Yaconelli sings a short Italian song very well and Hill supplies the typical medicine man humor, delivering laughs with every mouthful of words . . . Photography of the natural settings and the action are well done."

The same ballad, with a different name, *Rosita* (or maybe *Rosarita*), is sung by Yaconelli in Ken Maynard's *Lawless Riders*, made the year before, also in Lone Pine. Disputing their view, the weak warbling is no better with a varying title in *Lucky Terror.*

For its critique, the *National Board Of Review Magazine* concluded, "the action is brisk and interesting, the characters likable, and the photography remarkably good."

Promotional taglines:

"If you like trick riding, fancy shooting, and rollicking comedy—you'll like *Lucky Terror.*"

"Comedy with a capital C is the film fare offered by Hoot Gibson in his latest starring success, *Lucky Terror.*"

"*Lucky Terror* is filled with action, and crammed full of comedy . . . the type of picture in which Hoot Gibson has won his greatest success in the past."

And, indeed, his greatest success was in the past.

Pictures like *Lucky Terror* were aimed at America's many rural audiences, the ones who truly paid the freight for the movie industry. Preferring to focus on more prestigious cinema, today's film cognoscenti fail to appreciate this, or choose to ignore it. *Lucky Terror* is typical of the kind of programmer that deserves more respect. In any case, there are no figures available to reflect cost, profit, or loss that would help to assess box-office performance. But post-1935 Westerns were trending in the direction of singing cowboys not named Yaconelli, and there

Beginning in 1936 and continuing until after WWII, Hoot earned most of his living working rodeos and the few wild west shows still going. Here he is with a young fan in 1937.

Wallace Bro. Circus   1937

Hoot Gibson   JAN 1963   W.W.

was no second season for Walter Futter's modest Hoot Gibson series.

Something else we do not know. Passing for the Bonanza Mine is a forlorn metal shack high up in the hills, somewhere, evidently an area used for mining something, at some point, by someone near Lone Pine. The filmmakers make judicious use of an ore cart and tracks there. Intrepid researchers have yet to pinpoint its exact location, probably an area in the Cerro Gordo Mining District (southeast of Lone Pine near Keeler), the greatest silver and lead bullion producer in the history of California.

By 1938 Cerro Gordo was a ghost town, the mines all played out, much like motion picture options for Hoot Gibson. The star next travelled the sawdust circuit, performing trick riding and roping, and exploiting his celebrity status with endorsements and personal appearances. So many of his subsequent entrepreneurial activities failed: the dude ranch, the rodeos, selling chinchillas on TV in the 1950s, etc.

Through all of it, the Hooter never complained, never lost his optimism.

"You can't be a cowboy hero when you're well over fifty and losing your hair," Hoot laughed in remarks made in 1947 when he had fallen on hard times and was employed as a greeter for a Las Vegas hotel gaming casino. "I got nothin' to cry about. I made a lotta money. I blew it. This is a job and me 'n' my wife eat regular."

One highpoint for this non-singing cowboy was

Rested and ready for action! "Trail Blazers" Ken Maynard and Hoot Gibson ride again! In a reversal of form, the Hooter more often packed a six shooter throughout the Monogram series, which emphasized gunplay, because the stars were past the days when they could perform the physical action scenes expected in Westerns.

After three Trail Blazers films with only Hoot and Maynard, the producers decided to bring the younger, more athletic Bob Steele to the mix. After only two more films with the trio, Maynard's inability to get along with other members of the cast resulted in him being replaced with Chief Thundercloud, who finished out the series.

the lasting marriage in 1942 to a beautiful yodeler in his rodeo. Another was his pairing with pal Ken Maynard the following year for the Trail Blazers series at Monogram. These pictures, even then, were leveraged on nostalgia—the Over-the-Hill Gang rides again! In baseball, it would be like seeing Lou Gehrig and Babe Ruth coming back to the New York Yankees in their fifties or sixties, just hitting home runs all over the place to win every game.

"People like Westerns because they always know who's gonna win," Gibson told author Jon Tuska in 1959. "But it ain't that way in life."

Close friends Bob Nolan (of the Sons of the Pioneers) and Bob Steele (co-star of the Trail Blazers series) attended Gibson's funeral. So did a non-inebriated Ken Maynard, who lingered afterwards and spoke to many gathered outside the church. With tears in his eyes, holding a large white Stetson

at his side, he told long-time Poverty Row scenarist C. Jack Lewis, "Back in World War II, when almost everyone else was drafted, they offered us each $600 a picture to do the Trail Blazers series. We signed up and I made the comment, 'Looks like we better lose some weight.' Ol' Hooter popped back with, 'For the kinda money we're getting,' I ain't missin' no desserts.' He never took it seriously at all."

In a sidebar to Hoot Gibson's obituary, *The New York Times* wrote, "What amused the younger generation's fathers and grandfathers might not amuse anyone today. But the imaginary West of the pictures in which Mr. Gibson took a noble part stirs nostalgia in us just as does the equally imaginary West on which its romances were based."

So many humble but authentic and wonderful Lone Pine Westerns were produced by lowly independents, and consequently are orphan films

Hoot Gibson later in life signing autographs for fans at an event somehow involving Roy Rogers and Quaker Oats.

today. After Grand National was dissolved, Futter's Diversion negatives were acquired by a reissue house, Astor Pictures Corporation, and then syndicated in the early days of television by Atlantic Pictures. Next, the package was sold to Commonwealth United Television, but this time *Lucky Terror* was not syndicated over television. A license was arranged for Bill Blair's United Films, Inc. to exploit non-theatrical rental rights. Commonwealth United's library was next assigned to NTA, which eventually changed

Above: Gibson and Lona Andre have differing points of view in this scene from *Lucky Terror*. Below: Gibson and John Ford reminiscing between scenes of *The Horse Soldiers* (1959).

its name to Republic Entertainment Inc., which was acquired by Spelling Entertainment Group Inc., then in turn by Viacom, which now controls Paramount, which houses preprint material at the UCLA Film and Television Archive on real estate once owned by Hoot Gibson. But there are no elements in storage there for *Lucky Terror*. Not the camera negative, or any other preprint material. What happened to them? Who knows?

So preservation of the primary 35mm nitrate elements remains uncertain. There are, however, two 35mm nitrate exhibition prints stored at the Library of Congress. Will anyone make the case for restoration and preservation of orphan films like *Lucky Terror*? Why are they any less important, less reflective of popular culture in America than lofty, highbrow, studio-bound efforts celebrated by elite film critics and ivory tower film school professors to the exclusion of such efforts as *Lucky Terror*? They are not less important, less representative, are they?

We need Hoot Gibson, himself, now more than ever, to stand up, to say, "No! . . . And I'll tell ya the reason why!" □□□

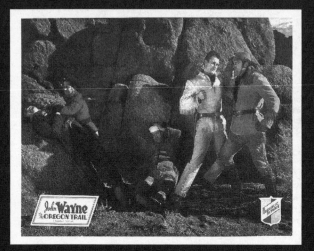

The fourth of John Wayne's eight B Westerns produced by Republic Pictures for release during the 1935–36 season, *The Oregon Trail* made the most of its limited budget with sturdily mounted, actionful exterior sequences shot in Lone Pine's Alabama Hills.

Directed by Scott Pembroke from an original screenplay attributed to Robert Emmett [Tansey], Jack Natteford, and Lindsley Parsons, the film boasted a strong cast that included silent-screen veterans Joe Girard, Frank Rice, Ben Hendricks, and E. H. Calvert. The Duke's leading lady was 18-year-old Ann Rutherford, and his long-time pal and stunt double Yakima Canutt took a key supporting role.

Wayne plays John Delmont, son of a Cavalry officer slain by renegades while traversing the Rocky Mountains. The ringleader steals the officer's credentials, then uses the dead man's name and authority to seize control of outlying settlements and build an empire of his own outside United States jurisdiction. Delmont joins a group of pioneers heading west on the Oregon Trail, eventually locates the renegade stronghold, and brings the villains to justice.

For reasons never determined, *The Oregon Trail* today is a lost movie. Never given theatrical reissue or sold to television, the film has not been seen since its release in 1936. Since Wayne's other Republics survive and have been revived in one form or another, *The Oregon Trail*'s disappearance is disturbing—especially since the synopsis and existing publicity stills suggest that it was an above-average entry in his superior 1935–36 series of B Westerns.

Usually, movies vanish or are suppressed for reasons related to underlying rights; if a film has been based on a work by a famous author and that author has not licensed rights for secondary usage, it is withdrawn with circulation following expiration of the initial licensing period. But *The Oregon Trail* was produced from an original screenplay, not adapted from a literary property created for another medium. Therefore, it should have survived among Republic's other holdings.

Moreover, since the company took pains to make Wayne's B Westerns available to exhibitors after he became a major star and transitioned to "A" pictures, it stands to reason that *The Oregon Trail* should have been reissued like the others. But it wasn't.

In the late 1970s a company called Nostalgia Merchant licensed the Republic film library with the intent of marketing 16mm prints of popular titles to private collectors. Nostalgia Merchant still owned non-theatrical rights to Republic movies when the home-video revolution began around that same time. In looking for original film elements to titles that might be big sellers, the Merchant's resident B–Western experts enlisted the aid of Ernest Kirkpatrick, faithful guardian of the treasures in Republic's vaults. Years of searching failed to turn up original negative material on *The Oregon Trail* either here in America or overseas where Republic maintained branches. A few odd 35mm reels of image eventually materialized, but nothing more.

From time to time it has been rumored that *The Oregon Trail* survives safe and sound, and recently Olive Films—the DVD company that currently owns video rights to Republic's output—grandly announced the film's imminent release in digital format. But then Olive's employees, like those of other companies before them, discovered that the cans marked *Oregon Trail* actually contained the 35mm elements to Republic's 1945 Sunset Carson Western of the same title. Olive's public-relations department sheepishly admitted its mistake and quietly canceled the release.

In any case, the loss of Wayne's version is a significant one. Surviving lobby cards and publicity stills indicate that extensive shooting was done in the Alabama Hills. In the film's absence we hope that Don Kelsen's photo essay presented on the following pages brings *The Oregon Trail* to life again, if only in the mind's eye. ☐☐☐

Professional photographer Don Kelsen has been documenting Festival activities in Lone Pine for a quarter-century and has spent countless hours wandering around the rocks of the Alabama Hills in pursuit of a passion— the rediscovery of famous movie locations. Using production stills and screen captures, he painstakingly searches for and selects a vantage point from which to duplicate some of the most spectacular background shots from our favorite Lone Pine films as illustrated in this small sample from his vast collection...

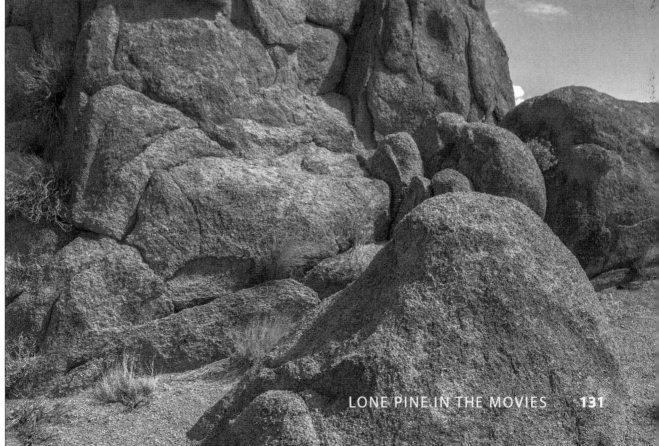

In my wandering searches for movie locations in the Alabama Hills, I have found that some are easy to find while others remain elusive. This site took many dusty trips to find and, as you can see, none of the foreground of the contemporary view is visible in the original movie scene. Guessing, I assume a camera platform was used both to film the scene and allow the studio photographer to create his version for the publicity still. Without having an elevated platform, the only available location for me to get the best contemporary recreation of the shot is the top of the rock you see in the foreground of the publicity still.

—*Don Kelsen*

Made in the USA
San Bernardino, CA
16 October 2016